Neville Goddard

Consciousness

The Giver Of All Gifts

Compiled and Edited
by
David Allen

Other books by David Allen

Neville Goddard's Interpretation Of Scripture, Unlocking The Secrets Of The Bible

The Power of I AM, Volumes 1, 2 and 3

Neville Goddard: Your Inner Conversations Are Creating Your World

The Neville Goddard Collection

and many more

Copyright © 2019

Copyright © 2019 by Shanon Allen / David Allen

All rights reserved. No part of this publication may be reproduced, distributed, or transmitted in any form or by any means, including photocopying, recording, or other electronic or mechanical methods, without the prior written permission of the publisher, except in the case of brief quotations embodied in critical reviews and certain other noncommercial uses permitted by copyright law.
Printed in the United States of America.

First Printing, August 2019

ISBN: 978-0-9995435-8-0

Visit Us At **NevilleGoddardBooks.com** for a complete listing of all our books and **1000's of Free Books to Read online and download.**

Copyright © 2019

Introduction

This is a compilation of extracts on consciousness from several of Neville's books - At Your Command, Your Faith Is Your Fortune, Prayer: The Art Of Believing, Out Of This World, Feeling Is The Secret, The Power of Awareness, Awakened Imagination And The Search, Seedtime And Harvest, Freedom For All, 1948 Classroom Lectures, Assumptions Harden Into Fact

As with all of Neville's teachings I suggest you read them every now and then. The reason being, that as you grow in your understanding you will start seeing what he was saying with new eyes (understanding). It will amaze you that as you do grow in understanding you will see things on subsequent readings that did not stand out to your conscious mind with the earlier readings. Should you choose to do this you will soon realize that you already have in your possession books that will enlighten you on how we create our reality.

I also believe that as you do grow in your understanding you will see why Joseph Murphy said of Neville... "Neville may eventually be recognized as one of the world's great mystics."

I already recognize him as such.

David Allen

Editors note: All scripture is italicized. I have not edited out the scripture references from Neville's books as some seem to believe. The first editions I have and the other first editions I have seen did not contain scripture references. They were added in later editions either by various editors or different publishers. For those who like to know verses they can easily be Googled.

Your Consciousness Is God, The Giver Of All Gifts

Neville Goddard - Consciousness: The Giver Of All Gifts

The law of consciousness is the only law of expression.

Consciousness is the one and only reality and is the foundation of the Bible.

Man's chief delusion is his conviction that there are causes other than his own state of consciousness.

Man is incapable of seeing other than the contents of his own consciousness.

Your life expresses one thing, and one thing only, your state of consciousness

Your consciousness is the mother-father, there is no other cause in the world.

Consciousness is the one and only reality. Therefore, we must form the object of our desire out of our own consciousness.

Consciousness is the way as well as the power which resurrects and expresses all that man will ever be conscious of being.

Your consciousness is the cause of your world.

Consciousness is the resurrecting power, resurrecting that which man is conscious of being.

Neville Goddard - Consciousness: The Giver Of All Gifts

Consciousness is the father that is drawing the manifestations of life unto you.

Consciousness is the way or door through which things appear.

If you have not the consciousness of the thing, you have not the cause or foundation upon which thing is erected.

Consciousness is the only reality and things but mirror that which you are in consciousness.

Consciousness is the way as well as the power which resurrects and expresses all that man will ever be conscious of being.

Consciousness is the one and only savior.

Consciousness is the cause of every expression in your life.

Your desire can be likened to a seed, and seeds contain within themselves both the power and the plan of self-expression. Your consciousness is the soil.

Consciousness is the door through which life reveals itself.

Consciousness is always objectifying itself.

Heaven is your consciousness.

Neville Goddard - Consciousness: The Giver Of All Gifts

Consciousness is the eternal light, which crystallizes only through the medium of your conception of yourself. Change your conception of yourself and you will automatically change the world in which you live.

Man does not realize that consciousness is the Father which does the work, so he attempts to express that which he is not conscious of being.

Your consciousness is the only living reality, the eternal head of creation.

Besides my consciousness there is no God. "Be still and know that I AM God" means that I should still the mind and know that consciousness is God.

Your consciousness is the one and only reality which animates and makes real that which you are conscious of being.

Your consciousness is the blood which makes all states living realities.

When you know that consciousness is the one and only reality, you will remain faithful to your vision, and by this sustained mental attitude confirm your gift of reality, and prove that you have the power to give reality to your desires that they may become visible concrete facts.

Consciousness is the cause as well as the substance of the entire world. So it is to consciousness that we must turn if we would discover the secret of creation.

Neville Goddard - Consciousness: The Giver Of All Gifts

Knowledge of the law of consciousness and the method of operating this law will enable you to accomplish all you desire in life.

It is of vital importance to understand clearly just what consciousness is. The reason lies in the fact that consciousness is the one and only reality, it is the first and only cause-substance of the phenomena of life.

A man's consciousness is all that he thinks and desires and loves, all that he believes is true and consents to.

A change of consciousness is necessary before you can change your outer world.

Until you realize that you are the Father (there is only one I AM, and your infinite self is that I AM), your will is always "I will be". Your consciousness of being is the Father's will. The mere wish without this consciousness is the "my will".

Once you know that consciousness is the only reality and is the sole creator of your particular world and have burnt this truth into your whole being, then you know that success or failure is entirely in your own hands.

When we understand that consciousness is the only reality, we know that it is the only creator. This means that your consciousness is the creator of your destiny.

Your state of consciousness is the spring of action, the directing force, and that which creates the supply.

Although normal consciousness is focused on the senses and is usually restricted to them, it is possible for man to pass through his sense fixation into any imaginal structure which he conceives and so fully occupy it, that it is more alive and more responsive than that on which his senses "stay his eye." If this were not true, man would be an automaton reflecting life, never affecting it.

To hear that which you desire does exist and you need only to accept it in consciousness is good news.

Where the consciousness is placed you do not have to take the physical body; it gravitates there in spite of you. Things happen to compel you to move in the direction where you are consciously dwelling

As we lift up our consciousness, our world reshapes itself in harmony with the level to which we have risen.

Now, if everything in my world depends upon a state of consciousness, it would be the height of insanity to seek the thing before I actually fix within myself the state on which the thing depends, for that which requires a state of consciousness to produce its effect cannot be effected without such a state of consciousness.

Can man decree a thing and have it come to pass? Most decidedly he can!

Man has always decreed that which has appeared in his world and is today decreeing that which is appearing in his world and shall continue to do so as long as man is conscious of being man.

Not one thing has ever appeared in man's world but what man decreed that it should. This you may deny, but try as you will you cannot disprove it, for this decreeing is based upon a changeless principle.

You do not command things to appear by your words or loud affirmations. Such vain repetition is more often than not confirmation of the opposite.

Decreeing is ever done in consciousness. That is; every man is conscious of being that which he has decreed himself to be. The dumb man without using words is conscious of being dumb. Therefore he is decreeing himself to be dumb.

When the Bible is read in this light you will find it to be the greatest scientific book ever written. Instead of looking upon the Bible as the historical record of an ancient civilization or the biography of the unusual life of Jesus, see it as a great psychological drama taking place in the consciousness of man.

Claim it as your own and you will suddenly transform your world from the barren deserts of Egypt to the promised land of Canaan.

(From At Your Command)

Consciousness is the resurrecting power, resurrecting that which man is conscious of being.

Man is ever out picturing that which he is conscious of being. This is the truth that makes man free, for man is always self-imprisoned or self-freed.

If you, the reader, will give up all of your former beliefs in a God apart from yourself, and claim God as your awareness of being, as Jesus and the prophets did, you will transform your world with the realization that,

"I and my father are one."

This statement,

"I and my father are one, but my father is greater than I,"

seems very confusing, but if interpreted in the light of what we have just said concerning the identity of God, you will find it very revealing.

Consciousness, being God, is as 'Father.' The thing that you are conscious of being is the 'son' bearing witness of his 'father.'

(From At Your Command)

Neville Goddard - Consciousness: The Giver Of All Gifts

"If any man should ever come, saying, 'Look here or look there,' believe them not, for the kingdom of God is within you."

Heaven is within you. Therefore, when it is recorded that

> *"He went unto his father,"*

it is telling you that he rose in consciousness to the point where he was just conscious of being, thus transcending the limitations of his present conception of himself, called 'Jesus.'

In the awareness of being all things are possible, he said,

> *"You shall decree a thing and it shall come to pass."*

This is his decreeing, rising in consciousness to the naturalness of being the thing desired. As he expressed it,

> *"And I, if I be lifted up, I shall draw all men unto me."*

If I be lifted up in consciousness to the naturalness of the thing desired I will draw the manifestation of that desire unto me. For he states,

> *"No man comes unto me save the father within me draws him, and I and my father are one."*

Therefore, consciousness is the father that is drawing the manifestations of life unto you.

You are, at this very moment, drawing into your world that which you are now conscious of being. Now you can see what is meant by,

> *"You must be born again."*

If you are dissatisfied with your present expression in life the only way to change it, is to take your attention away from that which seems so real to you and rise in consciousness to that which you desire to be.

Neville Goddard - Consciousness: The Giver Of All Gifts

You cannot serve two masters, therefore to take your attention from one state of consciousness and place it upon another is to die to one and live to the other.

(From At Your Command)

We are told,

"When you pray go within in secret and shut the door. And that which your father sees in secret, with that will he reward you openly."

We have identified the 'father' to be the awareness of being. We have also identified the 'door' to be the awareness of being.

So 'shutting the door' is shutting out that which 'I' AM now aware of being and claiming myself to be that which 'I' desire to be. The very moment my claim is established to the point of conviction, that moment I begin to draw unto myself the evidence of my claim.

Do not question the how of these things appearing, for no man knows that way. That is, no manifestation knows how the things desired will appear.

Consciousness is the way or door through which things appear. He said,

"I AM the way"

not 'I,' John Smith, am the way, but "I AM", the awareness of being, is the way through which the thing shall come.

The signs always follow. They never precede. Things have no reality other than in consciousness. Therefore, get the consciousness first and the thing is compelled to appear.

You are told,

"Seek ye first the kingdom of Heaven and all things shall be added unto you."

Get first the consciousness of the things that you are seeking and leave the things alone.

This is what is meant by

Neville Goddard - Consciousness: The Giver Of All Gifts

"Ye shall decree a thing and it shall come to pass."

Apply this principle and you will know what it is to

"prove me and see."

(From At Your Command)

"Go, tell no man."

That is, do not discuss your ambitions or desires with another for the other will only echo your present fears. Secrecy is the first law to be observed in realizing your desire.

The second, as we are told in the story of Mary, is to

"Magnify the Lord."

We have identified the Lord as your awareness of being. Therefore, to 'Magnify the Lord' is to revalue or expand one's present conception of one's self to the point where this revaluation becomes natural. When this naturalness is attained you give birth by becoming that which you are one with in consciousness.

The story of creation is given us in digest form in the first chapter of John.

"In the beginning was the word."

Now, this very second, is the 'beginning' spoken of. It is the beginning of an urge, a desire. 'The word' is the desire swimming around in your consciousness, seeking embodiment. The urge of itself has no reality, For, "I AM" or the awareness of being is the only reality. Things live only as long as I AM aware of being them; so to realize one's desire, the second line of this first verse of John must be applied. That is,

"And the word was with God."

The word, or desire, must be fixed or united with consciousness to give it reality. The awareness becomes aware of being the thing desired, thereby nailing itself upon the form or conception and giving life unto its conception, or resurrecting that which was heretofore a dead or unfulfilled desire.

(From At Your Command)

Neville Goddard - Consciousness: The Giver Of All Gifts

"Ye must be born again for except ye be born again ye cannot enter the kingdom of Heaven."

That is; except you leave behind you your present conception of yourself and assume the nature of the new birth, you will continue to out picture your present limitations.

The only way to change your expressions of life is to change your consciousness. For consciousness is the reality that eternally solidifies itself in the things round about you.

Man's world in its every detail is his consciousness out pictured. You can no more change your environment, or world, by destroying things than you can your reflection by destroying the mirror.

Your environment, and all within it, reflects that which you are in consciousness. As long as you continue to be that in consciousness so long will you continue to out picture it in your world.

(From At Your Command)

"The Lord is my shepherd; I shall not want"

is seen in its true light now to be your consciousness.

You could never be in want of proof or lack the evidence of that which you are aware of being.

This being true, why not become aware of being great; God-loving; wealthy; healthy; and all attributes that you admire?

It is just as easy to possess the consciousness of these qualities as it is to possess their opposites for you have not your present consciousness because of your world. On the contrary, your world is what it is because of your present consciousness.

(From At Your Command)

Neville Goddard - Consciousness: The Giver Of All Gifts

"I and my father are one but my father is greater than I."

You are one with your present conception of yourself. But you are greater than that which you are at present aware of being.

Before man can attempt to transform his world he must first lay the foundation,

> *"I AM the Lord."*

That is, man's awareness, his consciousness of being is God. Until this is firmly established so that no suggestion or argument put forward by others can shake it, he will find himself returning to the slavery of his former beliefs.

> *"If ye believe not that I AM he, ye shall die in your sins."*

That is, you shall continue to be confused and thwarted until you find the cause of your confusion.

When you have lifted up the son of man then shall you know that

> "I AM he",

that is, that I, John Smith, do nothing of myself, but my father, or that state of consciousness which I am now one with, does the works.

When this is realized every urge and desire that springs within you shall find expression in your world.

(From At Your Command)

Neville Goddard - Consciousness: The Giver Of All Gifts

"Behold I stand at the door and knock. If any man hear my voice and open the door I will come in to him and sup with him and he with me."

The "I" knocking at the door is the urge.

The door is your consciousness. To open the door is to become one with that that which is knocking by feeling oneself to be the thing desired.

To feel one's desire as impossible is to shut the door or deny this urge expression. To rise in consciousness to the naturalness of the thing felt is to swing wide the door and invite this one into embodiment.

That is why it is constantly recorded that Jesus left the world of manifestation and ascended unto his father.

Jesus, as you and I, found all things impossible to Jesus, as man. But having discovered his father to be the state of consciousness of the thing desired, he but left behind him the "Jesus consciousness" and rose in consciousness to that state desired and stood upon it until he became one with it.

As he made himself one with that, he became that in expression.

This is Jesus simple message to man: Men are but garments that the impersonal being, I AM, the presence that men call God, dwells in.

Each garment has certain limitations. In order to transcend these limitations and give expression to that which, as man, John Smith, you find yourself incapable of doing, you take your attention away from your present limitations, or John Smith conception of yourself, and merge yourself in the feeling of being that which you desire.

Just how this desire or newly attained consciousness will embody itself, no man knows.

For I, or the newly attained consciousness, has ways that ye know not of; its ways are past finding out.

Do not speculate as to the how of this consciousness embodying itself, for no man is wise enough to know the how.

Speculation is proof that you have not attained to the naturalness of being the thing desired and so are filled with doubts.

(From At Your Command)

You are told,

"He who lacks wisdom let him ask of God,
that gives to all liberally, and upbraideth not;
and it shall be given unto him.
But let him ask not doubting
for he who doubts is as a wave of the sea
that is tossed and battered by the winds.
And let not such a one think that
he shall receive anything from the Lord."

You can see why this statement is made, for only upon the rock of faith can anything be established. If you have not the consciousness of the thing, you have not the cause or foundation upon which thing is erected.

A proof of this established consciousness is given you in the words,

"Thank you, father."

When you come into the joy of thanksgiving so that you actually feel grateful for having received that which is not yet apparent to the senses, you have definitely become one in consciousness with the thing for which you gave thanks.

God (your awareness) is not mocked.

You are ever receiving that which you are aware of being and no man gives thanks for something which he has not received.

"Thank you father"

is not, as it is used by many today a sort of magical formula.

You need never utter aloud the words,

"Thank you, father."

In applying this principle as you rise in consciousness to the point where you are really grateful and happy for having received the thing desired, you automatically rejoice and give thanks inwardly.

You have already accepted the gift which was but a desire before you rose in consciousness, and your faith is now the substance that shall clothe your desire.

This rising in consciousness is the spiritual marriage where two shall agree upon being one and their likeness or image is established on earth.

(From At Your Command)

> **"For whatsoever ye ask in my name the same give I unto you."**

'Whatsoever' is quite a large measure. It is the unconditional. It does not state if society deems it right or wrong that you should ask it, it rests with you. Do you really want it? Do you desire it? That is all that is necessary.

> Life will give it to you is you ask
>
> *"in his name."*

His name is not a name that you pronounce with the lips. You can ask forever in the name of God or Jehovah or Christ Jesus and you will ask in vain.

'Name' means nature; so, when you ask in the nature of a thing, results ever follow.

To ask in the name is to rise in consciousness and become one in nature with the thing desired, rise in consciousness to the nature of the thing, and you will become that thing in expression.

> Therefore,
>
> *"what things soever ye desire, when ye pray, believe that ye receive them and ye shall receive them."*

(From At Your Command)

> *"Forgive if ye have aught against any,*
> *that your father also, which is in Heaven,*
> *may forgive you. But if ye forgive not,*
> *neither will your father forgive you."*

This may seem to be some personal God who is pleased or displeased with your actions but this is not the case.

Consciousness, being God, if you hold in consciousness anything against man, you are binding that condition in your world.

But to release man from all condemnation is to free yourself so that you may rise to any level necessary; there is therefore, no condemnation to those in Christ Jesus.

Therefore, a very good practice before you enter into your meditation is first to free every man in the world from blame.

For law is never violated and you can rest confidently in the knowledge that every man's conception of himself is going to be his reward.

So you do not have to bother yourself about seeing whether or not man gets what you consider he should get. For life makes no mistakes and always gives man that which man first gives himself.

(From At Your Command)

It is said,

"You believe in God. Believe also in me for I AM he."

Have the faith of God.

"He made himself one with God and found it not robbery to do the works of God."

Go you and do likewise. Yes, begin to believe your awareness, your consciousness of being to be God. Claim for yourself all the attributes that you have heretofore given an external God and you will begin to express these claims.

*"For I am not a God afar off.
I AM nearer than your hands and feet,
nearer than your very breathing."*

I AM your awareness of being. I AM that in which all that I shall ever be aware of being shall begin and end.

*"For before the world was I AM;
and when the world shall cease to be, I AM;
before Abraham was, I AM."*

This I AM is your awareness.

"Except the Lord build the house they labor in vain that build it."

'The Lord,' being your consciousness, except that which you seek is first established in your consciousness, you will labor in vain to find it.

All things must begin and end in consciousness.

(From At Your Command)

Neville Goddard - Consciousness: The Giver Of All Gifts

"No man"* (manifestation) *"comes unto me except the father within me draw him,"

and

"I and my father are one."

Believe this truth and you will be free. Man has always blamed others for that which he is and will continue to do so until he find himself as cause of all.

"I AM" comes not to destroy but to fulfill.

"I AM," the awareness within you, destroys nothing but ever fill full the molds or conception one has of one's self.

It is impossible for the poor man to find wealth in this world no matter how he is surrounded with it until he first claims himself to be wealthy.

For signs follow, they do not precede.

To constantly kick and complain against the limitations of poverty while remaining poor in consciousness is to play the fool's game. Changes cannot take place from that level of consciousness for life in constantly out picturing all levels.

Follow the example of the prodigal son. Realize that you, yourself brought about this condition of waste and lack and make the decision within yourself to rise to a higher level where the fatted calf, the ring, and the robe await your claim.

(From At Your Command)

Your desires contain within themselves the plan of self-expression.

So leave all judgments out of the picture and rise in consciousness to the level of your desire and make yourself one with it by claiming it to be so now.

For:

"My grace is sufficient for thee. My strength is made perfect in weakness."

Have faith in this unseen claim until the conviction is born within you that it is so. Your confidence in this claim will pay great rewards.

Just a little while and he, the thing desired, will come. But without faith it is impossible to realize anything. Through faith the worlds were framed because

"faith is the substance of the thing hoped for, the evidence of the thing not yet seen."

Don't be anxious or concerned as to results. They will follow just as surely as day follows night.

Look upon your desires, all of them, as the spoken words of God, and every word or desire a promise.

The reason most of us fail to realize our desires is because we are constantly conditioning them. Do not condition your desire. Just accept it as it comes to you. Give thanks for it to the point that you are grateful for having already received it, then go about your way in peace.

Such acceptance of your desire is like dropping seed, fertile seed, into prepared soil.

For when you can drop the thing desired in consciousness, confident that it shall appear, you have done all that is expected to you.

But, to be worried or concerned about the how of your desire maturing is to hold these fertile seeds in a mental grasp, and, therefore, never to have dropped them in the soil of confidence.

The reason men condition their desires is because they constantly judge after the appearance of being and see the things as real, forgetting that the only reality is the consciousness back of them.

To see things as real, is to deny that all things are possible to God (consciousness).

(From At Your Command)

Deny it if you will, it still remains a fact that consciousness is the only reality and things but mirror that which you are in consciousness.

So the heavenly state you are seeking will be found only in consciousness, for the kingdom of heaven is within you.

As the will of heaven is ever done on earth, you are today living in the heaven, that you have established within you. For here on this very earth, your heaven, reveals itself.

The kingdom of heaven really is at hand. now is the accepted time. So create a new heaven, enter into a new state of consciousness and a new earth will appear.

"The former things shall pass away. They shall not be remembered not come into mind any more. For behold, I," (your consciousness) "come quickly and my reward is with me."

I AM nameless but will take upon myself every name (nature) that you call me.

Remember it is you, yourself, that I speak of as 'me.' So every conception that you have of yourself, that is every deep conviction, you have of yourself is that which you shall appear as being,

for I AM not fooled;

"God is not mocked."

(From At Your Command)

Neville Goddard - Consciousness: The Giver Of All Gifts

> *"So shall My word be that goeth forth out of My mouth; it shall not return unto Me void, but it shall accomplish that which I please, and it shall prosper in the thing whereto I sent it."*

Man can decree a thing and it will come to pass.

Man has always decreed that which has appeared in his world. He is today decreeing that which is appearing in his world and he shall continue to do so as long as man is conscious of being man.

Nothing has ever appeared in man's world, but what man decreed that it should. This you may deny; but try as you will, you cannot disprove it for this decreeing is based upon a changeless principle.

Man does not command things to appear by his words, which are, more often than not, a confession of his doubts and fears.

Decreeing is ever done in consciousness.

Every man automatically expresses that which he is conscious of being. Without effort or the use of words, at every moment of time, man is commanding himself to be and to possess that which he is conscious of being and possessing.

This changeless principle of expression is dramatized in all the Bibles of the world.

The writers of our sacred books were illumined mystics, past masters in the art of psychology. In telling the story of the soul, they personified this impersonal principle in the form of a historical document both to preserve it and to hide it from the eyes of the uninitiated.

Today, those to whom this great treasure has been entrusted, namely, the priesthoods of the world, have forgotten that the Bibles are psychological dramas representing the consciousness of man; in their blind forgetfulness, they now teach their followers to worship its characters as men and women who actually lived in time and space.

When man sees the Bible as a great psychological drama, with all of its characters and actors as the personified qualities and attributes of his own consciousness, then and then only will the Bible reveal to him the light of its symbology.

(From Your Faith Is Your Fortune)

Neville Goddard - Consciousness: The Giver Of All Gifts

I AM; man's unconditioned awareness of being is revealed as Lord and Creator of every conditioned state of being.

If man would give up his belief in a God apart from himself, recognize his awareness of being to be God (this awareness fashions itself in the likeness and image of its conception of itself), he would transform his world from a barren waste to a fertile field of his own liking.

The day man does this he will know that he and his Father are one, but his Father is greater than he.

He will know that his consciousness of being is one with that which he is conscious of being, but that his unconditioned consciousness of being is greater than his conditioned state or his conception of himself.

When man discovers his consciousness to be the impersonal power of expression, which power eternally personifies itself in his conceptions of himself, he will assume and appropriate that state of consciousness which he desires to express; in so doing he will become that state in expression.

"Ye shall decree a thing and it shall come to pass"

can now be told in this manner:

You shall become conscious of being or possessing a thing and you shall express or possess that which you are conscious of being.

The law of consciousness is the only law of expression.

(From Your Faith Is Your Fortune)

"I AM the way".

"I AM the resurrection".

Consciousness is the way as well as the power which resurrects and expresses all that man will ever be conscious of being.

Turn from the blindness of the uninitiated man who attempts to express and possess those qualities and things which he is not conscious of being and possessing; and be as the illumined mystic who decrees, on the basis of this changeless law.

Consciously claim yourself to be that which you seek; appropriate the consciousness of that which you see; and you too will know the status of the true mystic, as follows:

I became conscious of being it. I am still conscious of being it. And I shall continue to be conscious of being it until that which I am conscious of being is perfectly expressed.

"Yes, I shall decree a thing and it shall come to pass."

(From Your Faith Is Your Fortune)

Neville Goddard - Consciousness: The Giver Of All Gifts

***"Ye shall know the truth,
and the truth shall make you free."***

The truth that sets man free is the knowledge that his consciousness is the resurrection and the life, that his consciousness both resurrects and makes alive all that he is conscious of being.

Apart from consciousness, there is neither resurrection nor life.

When man gives up his belief in a God apart from himself and begins to recognize his awareness of being to be God, as did Jesus and the prophets, he will transform his world with the realization,

"I and My Father are one"

but

"My Father is greater than I."

He will know that his consciousness is God and that which he is conscious of being is the Son bearing witness of God, the Father.

The conceiver and the conception are one, but the conceiver is greater than his conception.

"Before Abraham was, I AM."

Yes, I was aware of being before I became aware of being man, and in that day when I shall cease to be conscious of being man I shall still be conscious of being.

The consciousness of being is not dependent upon being anything. It preceded all conceptions of itself and shall be when all conceptions of itself shall cease to be.

(From Your Faith Is Your Fortune)

Neville Goddard - Consciousness: The Giver Of All Gifts

"I AM the beginning and the end".

That is, all things or conceptions of myself begin and end in me, but I, the formless awareness, remain forever.

Jesus discovered this glorious truth and declared Himself to be one with God, not the God that man had fashioned, for He never recognized such a God.

Jesus found God to be His awareness of being and so told man that the Kingdom of God and Heaven were within.

When it is recorded that Jesus left the world and went to His Father it is simply stating that He turned His attention from the world of the senses and rose in consciousness to that level which He desired to express.

There He remained until He became one with the consciousness to which He ascended. When He returned to the world of man, He could act with the positive assurance of that which He was conscious of being, a state of consciousness no one but Himself felt or knew that He possessed.

Man who is ignorant of this everlasting law of expression looks upon such happenings as miracles.

To rise in consciousness to the level of the thing desired and to remain there until such level becomes your nature is the way of all seeming miracles.

"And I, if I be lifted up, I shall draw all men unto Me"

If I be lifted up in consciousness to the naturalness of the thing desired, I shall draw the manifestation of that desire to me.

"No man comes unto Me save the Father within Me draws him",

and

Neville Goddard - Consciousness: The Giver Of All Gifts

"I and My Father are one."

My consciousness is the Father who draws the manifestation of life to me.

The nature of the manifestation is determined by the state of consciousness in which I dwell. I am always drawing into my world that which I am conscious of being.

If you are dissatisfied with your present expression of life, then you must be born again.

Rebirth is the dropping of that level with which you are dissatisfied and rising to that level of consciousness which you desire to express and possess.

You cannot serve two masters or opposing states of consciousness at the same time. Taking your attention from one state and placing it upon the other, you die to the one from which you have taken it and you live and express the one with which you are united.

Man cannot see how it would be possible to express that which he desires to be by so simple a law as acquiring the consciousness of the thing desired.

The reason for this lack of faith on the part of man is that he looks at the desired state through the consciousness of his present limitations. Therefore, he naturally sees it as impossible of accomplishment.

One of the first things man must realize is that it is impossible, in dealing with this spiritual law of consciousness,

> *"to put new wine into old bottles or new patches on old garments."*

That is, you cannot take any part of the present consciousness into the new state. For the state sought is complete in itself and needs no patching. Every level of consciousness automatically expresses itself.

Neville Goddard - Consciousness: The Giver Of All Gifts

To rise to the level of any state is to automatically become that state in expression. But, in order to rise to the level that you are not now expressing, you must completely drop the consciousness with which you are now identified.

Until your present consciousness is dropped, you will not be able to rise to another level.

Do not be dismayed. This letting go of your present identity is not as difficult as it might appear to be.

(From Your Faith Is Your Fortune)

"I AM the light of the world."

Man has so long worshipped the images of his own making that at first he finds this revelation blasphemous, but the day man discovers and accepts this principle as the basis of his life, that day man slays his belief in a God apart from himself.

The story of Jesus' betrayal in the Garden of Gethsemane is the perfect illustration of man's discovery of this principle.

We are told, the crowds armed with staves and lanterns sought Jesus in the dark of night. As they inquired after the whereabouts of Jesus (salvation), the voice answered,

"I AM";

whereupon the entire crowd fell to the ground. On regaining their composure, they again asked to be shown the hiding place of the savior and again the savior said,

*"I have told you that I AM, therefore
if ye seek Me, let all else go."*

Man in the darkness of human ignorance sets out on his search for God, aided by the flickering light of human wisdom.

As it is revealed to man that his I AM or awareness of being is his savior, the shock is so great, he mentally falls to the ground, for every belief that he has ever entertained, tumbles, as he realizes that his consciousness is the one and only savior.

The knowledge that his I AM is God, compels man to let all others go, for he finds it impossible to serve two Gods. Man cannot accept his awareness of being as God and at the same time believe in another deity.

With this discovery, man's human ear or hearing (understanding) is cut off by the sword of faith (Peter) as his perfect disciplined hearing (understanding) is restored by (Jesus) the knowledge that "I AM" is Lord and Savior.

Before man can transform his world, he must first lay this foundation or understanding.

> *"I AM the Lord."*

Man must know that his awareness of being is God. Until this is firmly established so that no suggestion or argument of others can shake him, he will find himself returning to the slavery of his former belief.

> *"If ye believe not that I AM He, ye shall die in your sins."*

Unless man discovers that his consciousness is the cause of every expression of his life, he will continue seeking the cause of his confusion in the world of effects, and so shall die in his fruitless search.

> *"I AM the vine and ye are the branches."*

Consciousness is the vine and that which you are conscious of being is as branches that you feed and keep alive.

Just as a branch has no life except it be rooted in the vine, likewise things have no life except you be conscious of them.

Just as a branch withers and dies if the sap of the vine ceases to flow towards it, so do things and qualities pass away if you take your attention from them; because your attention is the sap of life which sustains the expression of your life.

(From Your Faith Is Your Fortune)

Stop looking for the Master to come; he is with you always.

"I AM with you always, even unto the end of the world."

You will from time to time know yourself to be many things, but you need not be anything to know that you are. You can, if you so desire, disentangle yourself from the body you wear; in so doing, you realize that you are a faceless, formless awareness and not dependent on the form you are in your expression.

You will know that you are; you will also discover that this knowing that you are is God, the Father, which preceded all that you ever knew yourself to be. Before the world was, you were aware of being and so you were saying

"I AM",

and

"I AM"

will be, after all that you know yourself to be shall cease to be.

There are no Ascended Masters. Banish this superstition.

You will forever rise from one level of consciousness (master) to another; in so doing, you manifest the ascended level, expressing this newly acquired consciousness.

Consciousness being Lord and Master, you are the Master Magician conjuring that which you are now conscious of being.

"For God (consciousness) calleth those things which be not as though they were":

Things that are not now seen will be seen the moment you become conscious of being that which is not now seen.

Neville Goddard - Consciousness: The Giver Of All Gifts

This rising from one level of consciousness to another is the only ascension that you will ever experience. No man can lift you to the level you desire. The power to ascend is within yourself; it is your consciousness.

You appropriate the consciousness of the level you desire to express by claiming that you are now expressing such a level.

This is the ascension. It is limitless, for you will never exhaust your capacity to ascend.

Turn from the human superstition of ascension with its belief in masters, and find the only and everlasting master within yourself.

"Far greater is he that is in you than he that is in the world." Believe this. Do not continue in blindness, following after the mirage of masters. I assure you, your search can end only in disappointment.

"If you deny Me (your awareness of being), I shall deny you also."

"Thou shalt have no other God beside ME."

"Be still and know that I AM God."

"Come prove me and see if I will not open you the windows of Heaven and pour you out a blessing, that there shall not be room enough to receive it."

"Do you believe that the I AM is able to do this? Then claim ME to be that which you want to see poured out."

Claim yourself to be that which you want to be and that you shall be. Not because of masters will I give it unto you, but, because you have recognized me (yourself) to be that, I will give it unto you for "I AM" all things to all.

(From Your Faith Is Your Fortune)

Jesus, in stating that,

"He and His Father were one but that His Father was greater than He",

revealed His awareness (Father) to be one with that which He was aware of being. He found Himself as Father or awareness to be greater than that which He as Jesus was aware of being.

You and your conception of yourself are one. You are and always will be greater than any conception you will ever have of yourself.

Man fails to do the works of Jesus Christ because he attempts to accomplish them from his present level of consciousness.

You will never transcend your present accomplishments through sacrifice and struggle. Your present level of consciousness will only be transcended as you drop the present state and rise to a higher level.

You rise to a higher level of consciousness by taking your attention away from your present limitations and placing it upon that which you desire to be.
Do not attempt this in day-dreaming or wishful thinking, but in a positive manner. Claim yourself to be the thing desired. I AM that; no sacrifice, no diet, no human tricks.

All that is asked of you is to accept your desire. If you dare claim it, you will express it.

(From Your Faith Is Your Fortune)

"But whom say ye that I AM?"

"I AM the Lord; that is My name; and My glory will I not give to another."

"I AM the Lord, the God of all Flesh."

This I AM within you, the reader, this awareness, this consciousness of being, is the Lord, the God of all Flesh.

I AM is He that should come; stop looking for another.

As long as you believe in a God apart from yourself, you will continue to transfer the power of your expression to your conceptions, forgetting that you are the conceiver.

The power conceiving and the thing conceived are one but the power to conceive is greater than the conception. Jesus discovered this glorious truth when He declared,

"I and My Father are one, but My Father is greater than I."

The power conceiving itself to be man is greater than its conception. All conceptions are limitations of the conceiver.

"Before Abraham was, I AM." Before the world was, I AM.

Consciousness precedes all manifestations and is the prop upon which all manifestation rests. To remove the manifestations, all that is required of you, the conceiver, is to take your attention away from the conception.

Instead of "Out of sight, out of mind", it really is "Out of mind, out of sight".

(From Your Faith Is Your Fortune)

"I AM the door."

"I AM the way."

"I AM the resurrection and the life"

"No man (or manifestation) cometh unto My Father save by Me."

The I AM (your consciousness) is the only door through which anything can pass into your world.

Stop looking for signs. Signs follow; they do not precede. Begin to reverse the statement, "Seeing is believing", to "Believing is seeing".

Start now to believe, not with the wavering confidence based on deceptive external evidence but with an undaunted confidence based on the immutable law that you can be that which you desire to be. You will find that you are not a victim of fate, but a victim of faith (your own).

Only through one door can that which you seek pass into the world of manifestation.

"I AM the door".

Your consciousness is the door, so you must become conscious of being and having that which you desire to be and to have. Any attempt to realize your desires in ways other than through the door of consciousness makes you a thief and a robber unto yourself. Any expression that is not felt, is unnatural.

Before anything appears, God, I AM, feels itself to be the thing desired; and then the thing felt appears. It is resurrected; lifted out of the nothingness.

I AM wealthy, poor, healthy, sick, free or confined, were first of all impressions or conditions felt, before they became visible expressions.

Your world is your consciousness objectified. Waste no time trying to change the outside; change the within or the impression; and the without or expression will take care of itself.

When the truth of this statement dawns upon you, you will know that you have found the lost word or the key to every door.

I AM (your consciousness) is the magical lost word which was made flesh in the likeness of that which you are conscious of being.

"I AM He."

(From Your Faith Is Your Fortune)

Neville Goddard - Consciousness: The Giver Of All Gifts

"Behold! I (clothed in your desire), stand at the door (your consciousness) and knock. If you hear my voice and open unto me (recognize me as your savior), I will come in unto you and sup with you and you with me."

Just how my words, your desires, will be fulfilled, is not your concern. My words have a way ye know not of. Their ways are past finding out. All that is required of you is to believe. Believe your desires to be garments your savior wears.

Your belief that you are now that which you desire to be is proof of your acceptance of life's gifts.

You have opened the door for your Lord, clothed in your desire, to enter the moment you establish this belief.

"When ye pray, believe that ye have received and it shall be so."

"All things are possible to him who believes."

Make the impossible possible through your belief; and the impossible (to others) will embody itself in your world.

All men have had proof of the power of faith.

The faith that moves mountains is faith in yourself. No man has faith in God who lacks confidence in himself. Your faith in God is measured by your confidence in yourself.

"I and My Father are one",

man and his God are one, consciousness and manifestation are one.

(From Your Faith Is Your Fortune)

And God said,

"Let there be a firmament in the midst of the waters."

In the midst of all the doubts and changing opinions of others, let there be a conviction, a firmness of belief, and you shall see the dry land; your belief will appear.

The reward is to him that endureth unto the end. A conviction is not a conviction if it can be shaken.

Your desire will be as clouds without rain, unless you believe.

Your unconditioned awareness or I AM is the Virgin Mary who knew not a man and yet, unaided by man, conceived and bore a son. Mary, the unconditioned consciousness, desired and then became conscious of being the conditioned state which she desired to express, and in a way unknown to others, became it.

Go and do likewise; assume the consciousness of that which you desire to be and you, too, will give birth to your savior.

When the annunciation is made, when the urge or desire is upon you, believe it to be God's spoken word seeking embodiment through you.

"Go, tell no man of this holy thing that you have conceived".

Lock your secret within you and magnify the Lord, magnify or believe, your desire to be your savior, coming to be with you.

When this belief is so firmly established that you feel confident of results, your desire will embody itself. How it will be done, no man knows.

*I, your desire, have ways ye know not of;
my ways are past finding out.*

Neville Goddard - Consciousness: The Giver Of All Gifts

Your desire can be likened to a seed, and seeds contain within themselves both the power and the plan of self-expression. Your consciousness is the soil.

These seeds are successfully planted only if, after you have claimed yourself to be and to have that which you desire, you confidently await results without an anxious thought.

If I be lifted up in consciousness to the naturalness of my desire, I shall automatically draw the manifestation unto me.

Consciousness is the door through which life reveals itself. Consciousness is always objectifying itself.

To be conscious of being or possessing anything is to be or have that which you are conscious of being or possessing.

Therefore, lift yourself to the consciousness of your desire and you will see it automatically out picture itself.

To do this, you must deny your present identity.

"Let him deny himself".

You deny a thing by taking your attention away from it. To drop a thing, problem or ego from consciousness, you dwell upon God, God being I AM.

"Be still and know that I AM is God."

Believe, feel that I AM; know that this knowing one within you, your awareness of being, is God.

Close your eyes and feel yourself to be faceless, formless and without figure. Approach this stillness as though it were the easiest thing in the world to accomplish. This attitude will assure your success.

When all thought of problem or self is dropped from consciousness because you are now absorbed or lost in the feeling of just being I AM, then begin in this formless state to feel yourself to be that which you desire to be,

Neville Goddard - Consciousness: The Giver Of All Gifts

"I AM that I AM".

The moment you reach a certain degree of intensity so that you actually feel yourself to be a new conception, this new feeling or consciousness is established and in due time will personify itself in the world of form. This new perception will express itself as naturally as you now express your present identity.

To express the qualities of a consciousness naturally, you must dwell or live within that consciousness. Appropriate it by becoming one with it.

To feel a thing intensely, and then rest confidently that it is, makes the thing felt, appear within your world.

"I shall stand upon my watch and see the salvation of the Lord"

I shall stand firmly upon my feeling, convinced that it is so, and see my desire appear.

(From Your Faith Is Your Fortune)

Neville Goddard - Consciousness: The Giver Of All Gifts

"A man can receive nothing, except it be given him from Heaven"

Remember, heaven is your consciousness; the Kingdom of Heaven is within you. This is why you are warned against calling any man Father; your consciousness is the Father of all that you are.

Again you are told, *"Salute no man on the highway"* See no man as an authority.

Why should you ask man for permission to express, when you realize that your world, in its every detail, originated within you and is sustained by you as the only conceptional center?

Your whole world may be likened to solidified space mirroring the beliefs and acceptances as projected by a formless, faceless presence, namely, I AM.

Reduce the whole to its primordial substance and nothing would remain but you, a dimensionless presence, the conceiver.

The conceiver is a law apart. Conceptions under such law are not to be measured by past accomplishments or modified by present capacities for, without taking thought, the conception in a way unknown to man expresses itself.

Go within secretly and appropriate the new consciousness. Feel yourself to be it, and the former limitations shall pass away as completely and as easily as snow on a hot summer's day. You will not even remember the former limitations; they were never part of this new consciousness.

This rebirth Jesus referred to, when he said to Nicodemus, *"Ye must be born again,"* was nothing more than moving from one state of consciousness to another.

(From Your Faith Is Your Fortune)

Neville Goddard - Consciousness: The Giver Of All Gifts

Man, not knowing that his world is his individual consciousness out pictured, vainly strives to conform to the opinion of others rather than to conform to the one and only opinion existent, namely, his own judgment of himself.

When Jesus discovered His consciousness to be this wonderful law of self-government,

> He declared,

> *"And now I sanctify Myself that they also might be sanctified through the truth."*

He knew that consciousness was the only reality, that things objectified, were nothing more than different states of consciousness. Jesus warned His followers to seek first the Kingdom of Heaven (that state of consciousness that would produce the thing desired) and all things would be added to them.

> He also stated,

> *"I AM the truth."*

He knew that man's consciousness was the truth or cause of all that man saw his world to be.

Jesus realized that the world was made in the likeness of man. He knew that man saw his world to be what it was because man was what he was. In short, man's conception of himself determines that which he sees his world to be.

> *"All things are made by God (consciousness) and without him there is nothing made that is made."*

Creation is judged good and very good because it is the perfect likeness of that consciousness which produced it.

To be conscious of being one thing and then see yourself expressing something other than that which you are conscious of being is a violation of the law of being; therefore, it would not be good.

The law of being is never broken; man ever sees himself expressing that which he is conscious of being. Be it good, bad or indifferent, it is nevertheless a perfect likeness of his conception of himself; it is good and very good.

Not only are all things made by God, all things are made of God. All are the offspring of God. God is one. Things or divisions are the projections of the one.

God being one, He must command Himself to be the seeming other for there is no other.

(From Your Faith Is Your Fortune)

"I AM the light of the world,"

crystallizing into the form of my conception of myself.

Consciousness is the eternal light, which crystallizes only through the medium of your conception of yourself. Change your conception of yourself and you will automatically change the world in which you live.

Do not try to change people; they are only messengers telling you who you are. Revalue yourself and they will confirm the change.

Now you will realize why Jesus sanctified Himself instead of others, why to the pure all things are pure, why in Christ Jesus (the awakened consciousness) there is no condemnation. Awake from the sleep of condemnation and prove the principle of life. Stop not only your judgment of others but your condemnation of yourself.

Hear the revelation of the enlightened,

"I know and am persuaded by the Lord Christ Jesus that there is nothing unclean of itself, but to him that seeth anything to be unclean to him it is unclean,"

and again,

"Happy is the man who condemneth himself not in that which he alloweth."

Stop asking yourself whether or not you are worthy or unworthy to claim yourself to be that which you desire to be. You will be condemned by the world only as long as you condemn yourself.

You do not need to work out anything. The works are finished.

The principle by which all things are made and without which there is not anything made that is made, is eternal.

Neville Goddard - Consciousness: The Giver Of All Gifts

You are this principle.

Your awareness of being is this everlasting law.

You have never expressed anything that you were not aware of being and you never will.

Assume the consciousness of that which you desire to express. Claim it, until it becomes a natural manifestation. Feel it and live within that feeling, until you make it your nature.

(From Your Faith Is Your Fortune)

"Leave all and follow me."

In the face of seemingly mountainous obstacles, claim your freedom.

The consciousness of freedom is the Father of freedom. It has a way of expressing itself which no man knows.

"Ye shall not need to fight in this battle. Set yourself, stand still, and see the salvation of the Lord with you."

"I AM the Lord."

I AM (your consciousness) is the Lord. The consciousness that the thing is done, that the work is finished, is the Lord of any situation.

Listen carefully to the promise,

"Ye shall not need to fight in this battle: Set yourself, stand still, and see the salvation of the Lord with you."

With you!

That particular consciousness with which you are identified is the Lord of the agreement. He will without assistance establish the thing agreed upon on earth.

Can you, in the face of the army of reasons why a thing cannot be done, quietly enter into an agreement with the Lord that it is done?

Can you, now that you have found the Lord to be your awareness of being, become aware that the battle is won? Can you, no matter how near and threatening the enemy seems to be, continue in your confidence, standing still, knowing that the victory is yours? If you can, you will see the salvation of the Lord.

(From Your Faith Is Your Fortune)

Neville Goddard - Consciousness: The Giver Of All Gifts

In Revelations, it is recorded that a new heaven and new earth shall appear.

John, shown this vision, was told to write,

"It is done."

Heaven is your consciousness and earth its solidified state.

Therefore, accept as did John . . "It is done".

All that is required of you who seek a change is to rise to a level of that which you desire; without dwelling upon the manner of expression, record that 'it is done' by feeling the naturalness of being it.

Here is an analogy that might help you to see this mystery.

Suppose you entered a motion picture theatre just as the feature picture came to its end. All that you saw of the picture was the happy ending. Because you wanted to see the entire story, you waited for it to unfold again. With the anticlimactic sequence, the hero is displayed as accused, surrounded by false evidence, and all that goes to wring tears from the audience.

But, you, secure in the knowledge of the ending, remain calm with the understanding that, regardless of the seeming direction of the picture, the end has already been defined.

In like manner, go to the end of that which you seek; witness the happy end of it by consciously feeling you express and possess that which you desire to express and possess; and you, through faith, already understanding the end, will have confidence born of this knowledge.

This knowledge will sustain you through the necessary interval of time that it takes the picture to unfold.

Ask no help of man;

feel,

Neville Goddard - Consciousness: The Giver Of All Gifts

"It is done",

by consciously claiming yourself to be, now, that which as man, you hope to be.

(From Your Faith Is Your Fortune)

When you say,

"I AM",

you are declaring yourself to be, first person, present tense; there is no future. To know that I AM is to be conscious of being. Consciousness is the only door. Unless you are conscious of being that which you seek, you seek in vain.

If you judge after appearances, you will continue to be enslaved by the evidence of your senses.

To break this hypnotic spell of the senses, you are told,

"Go within and shut the door"

The door of the senses must be tightly shut before your new claim can be honored. Closing the door of the senses is not as difficult as it appears to be at first. It is done without effort.

It is impossible to serve two masters at the same time.

The master man serves is that which he is conscious of being.

I AM Lord and Master of that which I AM conscious of being. It is no effort for me to conjure poverty if I am conscious of being poor.

My servant (poverty), is compelled to follow me (consciousness of poverty), as long as I AM (the Lord), conscious of being poor.

Instead of fighting against the evidence of the senses, you claim yourself to be that which you desire to be. As your attention is placed on this claim, the doors of the senses automatically close against your former master (that which you were conscious of being).

Neville Goddard - Consciousness: The Giver Of All Gifts

As you become lost in the feeling of being, that which you are now claiming to be true of yourself, the doors of the senses once more open, revealing your world to be the perfect expression of that which you are conscious of being.

Let us follow the example of Jesus who realized, as man, He could do nothing to change His present picture of lack. He closed the door of His senses against His problem and went to His Father, the one to Whom all things are possible.

Having denied the evidence of His senses, He claimed Himself, to be all that, a moment before, His senses told him, He was not.

Knowing that consciousness expresses its likeness on earth, He remained in the claimed consciousness until the doors (His senses) opened and confirmed the rulership of the Lord.

Remember,

"I AM is Lord of all."

Never again use the will of man which claims,

"I will be".

Be as resigned as Jesus and claim,

"I AM that".

(From Your Faith Is Your Fortune)

Neville Goddard - Consciousness: The Giver Of All Gifts

Man feels so secure in his man-made laws, opinions and beliefs that he invests them with an authority they do not possess.

Satisfied that his knowledge is all, he remains unaware that all outward appearances are but states of mind externalized.

When he realizes that the consciousness of a quality externalizes that quality without the aid of any other or many values, and establishes the one true value, his own consciousness.

> *"The Lord is in His holy temple."*

> Consciousness dwells within that which it is conscious of being.

> I AM is the Lord, and man, his temple.

Knowing that consciousness objectifies itself, man must forgive all men for being that which they are.

He must realize that all are expressing, without the aid of another, that which they are conscious of being.

Peter, the enlightened or disciplined man, knew that a change of consciousness would produce a change of expression. Instead of sympathizing with the beggars of life at the temple's gate, he declared,

> *"Silver and gold have I none (for thee), but such as I have (the consciousness of freedom), give I unto thee."*

> *"Stir up the gift within you"*

Stop begging and claim yourself to be that which you decide to be. Do this and you too will jump from your crippled world into the world of freedom, singing praises to the Lord, I AM.

> *"Far greater is He that is in you than he that is in the world"*

This is the cry of everyone who finds his awareness of being to be God.

Your recognition of this fact will automatically cleanse the temple, your consciousness, of the thieves and robbers, restoring to you that dominion over things, which you lost the moment you forgot the command,

"Thou shalt have no other God beside ME".

(From Your Faith Is Your Fortune)

Neville Goddard - Consciousness: The Giver Of All Gifts

*"**Let every man take heed how he buildeth thereon. For other foundations can no man lay than that is laid, which is Jesus Christ.** Now if man build upon this foundation gold, silver, precious stones, wood, hay, stubble; every man's work shall be made manifest; for the day shall declare it."*

The foundation of all expression is consciousness.

Try as man will, he cannot find a cause of manifestation other than his consciousness of being. Man thinks he has found the cause of disease in germs, the cause of war in conflicting political ideologies and greed.

All such discoveries of man, catalogued as the essence of Wisdom, are foolishness in the eyes of God. There is only one power and this power is God (consciousness).

It kills; it makes alive; it wounds; it heals; it does all things, good, bad or indifferent.

Man moves in a world that is nothing more or less than his consciousness objectified. Not knowing this, he wars against his reflections while he keeps alive the light and the images which project the reflections.

"I AM the light of the world."

"I AM (consciousness) is the light".

That which I am conscious of being (my conception of myself) such as

"I AM rich", "I AM healthy", "I AM free",

are the images.

The world is the mirror magnifying all that I AM conscious of being.

Stop trying to change the world since it is only the mirror.

Neville Goddard - Consciousness: The Giver Of All Gifts

Man's attempt to change the world by force is as fruitless as breaking a mirror in the hope of changing his face. Leave the mirror and change your face. Leave the world alone and change your conceptions of yourself. The reflection then will be satisfactory.

Freedom or imprisonment, satisfaction or frustration can only be differentiated by the consciousness of being.

Regardless of your problem, its duration or its magnitude, careful attention to these instructions will in an amazingly short time, eliminate, even the memory of the problem.

Ask yourself this question: "How would I feel if I were free?" The very moment you sincerely ask this question, the answer comes.

No man can tell another the satisfaction of his desire fulfilled. It remains for each within himself to experience the feeling and joy of this automatic change of consciousness. The feeling or thrill that comes to one in response to his self-questioning is the Father state of consciousness or Foundation Stone upon which the conscious change is built.

Just how this feeling will embody itself no one knows, but it will; the Father (consciousness) has ways that no man knows; it is the unalterable law.

All things express their nature. As you wear a feeling, it becomes your nature. It might take a moment or a year, it is entirely dependent upon the degree of conviction.

As doubts vanish and you can feel

"I AM this",

you begin to develop the fruit or the nature of the thing you are feeling yourself to be.

When a person buys a new hat or pair of shoes, he thinks everyone knows that they are new. He feels unnatural with his newly acquired apparel until it becomes a part of him.

The same applies to the wearing of the new states of consciousness.

When you ask yourself the question, "How would I feel if my desire were at this moment realized?" the automatic reply, until it is properly conditioned by time and use, is actually disturbing.

The period of adjustment to realize this potential of consciousness is comparable to the newness of the wearing apparel.

Not knowing that consciousness is ever out picturing itself in conditions round about you, like Lot's wife, you continually look back upon your problem and again become hypnotized by its seeming naturalness.

Heed the words of Jesus (salvation):

"Leave all and follow Me."

"Let the dead bury the dead."

Your problem might have you so hypnotized by its seeming reality and naturalness that you find it difficult to wear the new feeling or consciousness of your savior.

You must assume this garment if you would have results. The stone (consciousness) which the builders rejected (would not wear) is the chief cornerstone, and other foundations no man can lay.

(From Your Faith Is Your Fortune)

> **"To him that hath not, it shall be taken from him and added to the one that hath",**

the rich get richer and the poor get poorer. You can only magnify that which you are conscious of being.

All things gravitate to that consciousness with which they are in tune.

Likewise, all things disentangle themselves from that consciousness with which they are out of tune.

Divide the wealth of the world equally among all men and in a short time, this equal division will be as originally disproportioned. Wealth will find its way back into the pockets of those from whom it was taken.

Instead of joining the chorus of the have-nots who insist on destroying those who have, recognize this changeless law of expression.

Consciously define yourself as that which you desire.

Once defined, your conscious claim established, continue in this confidence until the reward is received.

As surely as the day follows the night, any attribute, consciously claimed, will manifest itself.

Thus, that which to the sleeping orthodox world is a cruel and unjust law becomes to the enlightened one of the most merciful and just statements of truth.

> *"I AM come not to destroy but to fulfill."*

Nothing is actually destroyed. Any seeming destruction is a result of a change in consciousness.

Consciousness ever fills full the state in which it dwells.

The state from which consciousness is detached seems to those not familiar with this law to be destructive.

However, this is only preparatory to a new state of consciousness.

Claim yourself to be that which you want filled full.

"Nothing is destroyed. All is fulfilled."

"To him that hath it shall be given"

(From Your Faith Is Your Fortune)

"I AM the resurrection and the life of the desire".

I AM (your awareness of being) is the power resurrecting and making alive that which in your awareness you desire to be.

> *"Two shall agree on touching anything
> and I shall establish it on earth"*

The two agreeing are you (your awareness . . the consciousness desiring) and the thing desired.

When this agreement is attained, the crucifixion is completed; two have crossed or crossified each other.

I AM and THAT,

consciousness and that which you are conscious of being, have joined and are one; I AM now nailed or fixed in the belief that I AM this fusion.

Jesus or I AM is nailed upon the cross of that. The nail that binds you upon the cross is the nail of feeling. The mystical union is now consummated and the result will be the birth of a child or the resurrection of a son bearing witness of his Father. Consciousness is united to that which it is conscious of being.

The world of expression is the child confirming this union. The day you cease to be conscious of being that which you are now conscious of being, that day your child or expression shall die and return to the bosom of his father, the faceless, formless awareness.

All expressions are the results of such mystical unions. So the priests are correct when they say that true marriages are made in heaven and can only be dissolved in heaven. But let me clarify this statement by telling you that heaven is not a locality; it is a state of consciousness.

The Kingdom of Heaven is within you.

(From Your Faith Is Your Fortune)

Neville Goddard - Consciousness: The Giver Of All Gifts

In Heaven (consciousness) God is touched by that which he is aware of being.

"Who has touched me?
For I perceive virtue has gone out of me"

The moment this touching (feeling) takes place, there is an offspring or going-out-of-me into visibility taking place.

The day man feels

"I AM free", "I AM wealthy", "I AM strong",

God (I AM) is touched or crucified by these qualities or virtues. The results of such touching or crucifying will be seen in the birth or resurrection of the qualities felt, for man must have visible confirmation of all that he is conscious of being.

Now you will know why man or manifestation is always made in the image of God.

Your awareness imagines and out pictures all that you are aware of being.

"I AM the Lord and besides me there is no God."

"I AM the Resurrection and the Life."

You shall become fixed in the belief that you are that which you desire to be. Before you have any visible proof that you are, you will, from the deep conviction which you have felt fixed within you, know that you are; and so, without waiting for the confirmation of your senses, you will cry, *"It is finished"*

Then, with a faith born of the knowledge, of this changeless law, you will be as one dead and entombed; you will be still and unmoved in your conviction and confident that you will resurrect the qualities that you have fixed and are feeling within you.

(From Your Faith Is Your Fortune)

Neville Goddard - Consciousness: The Giver Of All Gifts

"And as we have borne the image of the earthly, we shall also bear the image of the heavenly."

Your consciousness or your I AM is the unlimited potential upon which impressions are made. I'm-pressions are defined states pressed upon your I AM.

Your consciousness or your I AM can be likened to a sensitive film. In the virgin state, it is potentially unlimited. You can impress or record a message of love or a hymn of hate, a wonderful symphony or discordant jazz. It does not matter what the nature of the impression might be; your I AM will, without a murmur, willingly receive and sustain all impressions. Your consciousness is the one referred to in Isaiah 53:3-7.

> *"He is despised and rejected of men; a man of sorrows, and acquainted with grief: and we hid as it were our faces from Him, He was despised, and we esteemed Him not".*

> *"Surely He hath borne our grieves, and carried our sorrows: yet we did esteem Him stricken, smitten of God, and afflicted".*

> *"But He was wounded for our transgressions, He was bruised for our iniquities: the chastisement of our peace was upon him; and with his stripes we are healed".*

> *"All we like sheep have gone astray; we have turned everyone to his own way; and the Lord hath laid on Him the iniquity of us all".*

> *"He was oppressed, and He was afflicted, yet He opened not his mouth: He is brought as a lamb to the slaughter and as a sheep before her shearers is dumb, so He openeth not His mouth."*

Your unconditioned consciousness is impersonal; it is no respecter of persons. Without thought or effort, it automatically expresses every impression that is registered upon it. It does not object to any impression that is placed upon it for; although it is capable of receiving and expressing any and all defined states, it remains forever an immaculate and an unlimited potential.

(From Your Faith Is Your Fortune)

INTERVAL OF TIME
(Entire Chapter - Your Faith Is Your Fortune)

"Let not your heart be troubled; ye believe in God, believe also in Me. In My Father's house are many mansions; if it were not so, I would have told you. I go to prepare a place for you. And if I go and prepare a place for you, I will come again, and receive you unto Myself; that where I am, there ye may be also."

The ME in whom you must believe is your consciousness, the I AM; it is God. It is also the Father's house containing within itself all conceivable states of consciousness.

Every conditioned state of consciousness is called a mansion.

This conversation takes place within yourself.

Your I AM, the unconditioned consciousness, is the Christ Jesus speaking to the conditioned self or the John Smith consciousness. "I AM John", from a mystical point of view, is two beings, namely, Christ and John.

So I go to prepare a place for you, moving from your present state of consciousness into that state desired. It is a promise by your Christ or awareness of being to your present conception of yourself that you will leave your present consciousness and appropriate another.

Man is such a slave to time that, if after he has appropriated a state of consciousness which is not now seen by the world and it, the appropriated state, does not immediately embody itself, he loses faith in his unseen claim; forthwith he drops it and returns to his former static state of being.

Because of this limitation of man, I have found it very helpful to employ a specified interval of time in making this journey into a prepared mansion.

"Wait but a little while."

Neville Goddard - Consciousness: The Giver Of All Gifts

We have all catalogued the different days of the week, months of the year and seasons.

By this, I mean you and I have said time and again, "Why, today feels just like Sunday" or " Monday" or " Saturday". We have also said in the middle of Summer, "Why, this feels and looks like the Fall of the year".

This is positive proof that you and I have definite feelings associated with these different days, months and seasons of the year. Because of this association, we can at any time consciously dwell in that day or season which we have selected.

Do not selfishly define this interval in days and hours because you are anxious to receive it, but simply remain in the conviction that it is done; time, being purely relative, should be eliminated entirely . . and your desire will be fulfilled.

This ability to dwell at any point in time permits us to employ time in our travel into the desired mansion.

Now I (consciousness) go to a point in time and there prepare a place. If I go to such a point in time and prepare a place, I shall return to this point in time where I have left; and I shall pick up and take you with me into that place which I have prepared, that where I AM, there ye may also be.

>Let me give you an example of this travel.

Suppose you had an intense desire. Like most men who are enslaved by time, you might feel that you could not possibly realize so large a desire in a limited interval.

But admitting that all things are possible to God, believing God to be the ME within you or your consciousness of being, you can say,

"As John, I can do nothing; but since all things are possible to God and God I know to be my consciousness of being, I can realize my desire in a little while. How my desire will be realized I do not (as John) know, but by the very law of my being I do know that it shall be".

With this belief firmly established, decide what would be a relative, rational interval of time in which such a desire could be realized. Again, let me remind you not to shorten the interval of time because you are anxious to receive your desire; make it a natural interval.

No one can give you the time interval. Only you can say what the natural interval would be to you. The interval of time is relative, that is, no two individuals would give the same measurement of time for the realization of their desire.

Time is ever conditioned by man's conception of himself.

Confidence in yourself as determined by conditioned consciousness always shortens the interval of time.

If you were accustomed to great accomplishments, you would give yourself a much shorter interval in which to accomplish your desire than the man schooled in defeat.

If today were Wednesday and you decided that it would be quite possible for your desire to embody a new realization of yourself by Sunday, then Sunday becomes the point in time that you would visit.

To make this visit, you shut out Wednesday and let in Sunday. This is accomplished by simply feeling that it is Sunday. Begin to hear the church bells; begin to feel the quietness of the day and all that Sunday means to you; actually feel that it is Sunday.

When this is accomplished, feel the joy of having received that which on Wednesday was but a desire. Feel the complete thrill of having received it, and then return to Wednesday, the point in time you left behind you.

In doing this, you created a vacuum in consciousness by moving from Wednesday to Sunday. Nature, abhorring vacuums, rushes in to fill it, thereby fashioning a mold in the likeness of that which you potentially create, namely, the joy of having realized your defined desire.

As you return to Wednesday, you will be filled with a joyful expectancy, because you have established the consciousness of that which must take place the following Sunday.

As you walk through the interval of Thursday, Friday and Saturday, nothing disturbs you regardless of conditions, because you predetermined that which you would be on the Sabbath and that remains an unalterable conviction.

Having gone before and prepared the place, you have returned to John and are now taking him with you through the interval of three days into the prepared place that he might share your joy with you,

"for where I AM, there ye may also be."

(From Your Faith Is Your Fortune)

> ***"And God said, Let Us make man in
> Our image, after Our likeness."***

Having discovered God to be our awareness of being and this unconditioned changeless reality (the I AM) to be the only creator, let us see why the Bible records a trinity as the creator of the world.

In the 26th verse of the first chapter of Genesis, it is stated,

"And God said, Let Us make man in Our image."

The churches refer to this plurality of Gods as God the Father, God the Son and God the Holy Spirit.

What is meant by "God the Father, God the Son and God the Holy Spirit" they have never attempted to explain, for they are in the dark concerning this mystery.

The Father, Son and Holy Spirit are three aspects or conditions of the unconditioned awareness of being called God.

The consciousness of being precedes the consciousness of being something. That unconditioned awareness which preceded all states of awareness is God . . I AM.

The three conditioned aspects or divisions of itself can best be told in this manner:

The receptive attitude of mind is that aspect which receives impressions and therefore may be likened to a womb or Mother.

That which makes the impression is the male or pressing aspect and is therefore known as Father.

The impression in time becomes an expression, which expression is ever the likeness and image of the impression; therefore this objectified aspect is said to be the Son bearing witness of his Father-Mother.

Neville Goddard - Consciousness: The Giver Of All Gifts

An understanding of this mystery of the trinity enables the one who understands it to completely transform his world and fashion it to his own liking.

(From Your Faith Is Your Fortune)

Millions of prayers are daily unanswered, because man prays to a God, who does not exist.

Consciousness being God, one must seek in consciousness, for the thing desired, by assuming the consciousness, of the quality desired. Only as one does this, will his prayers be answered.

To be conscious of being poor while praying for riches, is to be rewarded with that which you are conscious of being, namely, poverty.

Prayers, to be successful, must be claimed and appropriated. Assume the positive consciousness of the thing desired.

With your desire defined, quietly go within and shut the door behind you. Lose yourself in your desire; feel yourself to be one with it; remain in this fixation until you have absorbed the life and name by claiming and feeling yourself to be and to have that which you desired.

When you emerge from the hour of prayer, you must do so, conscious of being and possessing, that which you heretofore desired.

(From Your Faith Is Your Fortune)

Neville Goddard - Consciousness: The Giver Of All Gifts

"Then the LORD God formed man of dust from the ground, and breathed into his nostrils the breath of life; and man became a living being."

"As thou knowest not what is the way of the spirit, nor how the bones do grow in the womb of her that is with child: even so thou knowest not the works of God who maketh all/Just as you don't know how the breath of life enters the limbs of a child within its mother's womb, you also don't understand how God, who made everything, works."

"And it came to pass after these things, that the son of the woman, the mistress of the house, fell sick; and his sickness was so sore, that there was no breath left in him."

"And he (Elisha) went up, and lay upon the child, and put his mouth upon his mouth, and his eyes upon his eyes, and his hands upon his hands: and stretched himself upon the child; and the flesh of the child waxed warm."

"But after the three and a half days, the breath of life from God came into them, and they stood on their feet; and great fear fell upon those who were watching them."

Did the Prophet Elijah really restore to life the dead child of the Widow?

This story, along with all the other stories of the Bible, is a psychological drama which takes place in the consciousness of man.

The Widow symbolizes every man and woman in the world; the dead child represents the frustrated desires and ambitions of man; while the prophet, Elijah, symbolizes the God power within man, or man's awareness of being.

The story tells us that the prophet took the dead child from the Widow's bosom and carried him into an upper room. As he entered this upper room he closed the door behind them; placing the child upon a bed, he breathed life into him; returning to the mother, he gave her the child and said,

Neville Goddard - Consciousness: The Giver Of All Gifts

"Woman, thy son liveth"

Man's desires can be symbolized as the dead child. The mere fact that he desires, is positive proof that the thing desired is not yet a living reality in his world. He tries in every conceivable way to nurse this desire into reality, to make it live, but finds in the end that all attempts are fruitless.

Most men are not aware of the existence of the infinite power within themselves as the prophet.

They remain indefinitely with a dead child in their arms, not realizing that the desire is the positive indication of limitless capacities for its fulfillment.

Let man once recognize that his consciousness is a prophet who breathes life into all that he is conscious of being, and he will close the door of his senses against his problem and fix his attention, solely on that which he desires, knowing that by so doing, his desires are certain to be realized.

He will discover recognition to be the breath of life, for he will perceive, as he consciously claims himself to be now expressing or possessing all he desires to be or to have, that he will be breathing the breath of life into his desire. The quality claimed for the desire (in a way unknown to him) will begin to move and become a living reality in his world.

Yes, the Prophet Elijah lives forever as man's limitless consciousness of being, the widow as his limited consciousness of being and the child as that which he desires to be.

(From Your Faith Is Your Fortune)

Look upon your desires as the spoken words of God and every word of prophecy of that which you are capable of being.

Do not question whether you are worthy or unworthy to realize these desires.

Accept them as they come to you. Give thanks for them as though they were gifts. Feel happy and grateful for having received such wonderful gifts. Then go your way in peace. Such simple acceptance of your desires is like the dropping of fertile seed into an ever-prepared soil.

When you drop your desire in consciousness as a seed, confident that it shall appear in its full-blown potential, you have done all that is expected of you.

To be worried or concerned about the manner of their unfoldment is to hold these fertile seeds in a mental grasp and, therefore, to prevent them from really maturing to full harvest.

Don't be anxious or concerned as to results. Results will follow just as surely as day follows night. Have faith in this planting, until the evidence is manifest to you, that it is so. Your confidence in this procedure will pay great rewards. You wait but a little while in the consciousness of the thing desired; then suddenly, and when you least expect it, the thing felt becomes your expression.

Life is no respecter of persons and destroys nothing; it continues to keep alive that which man is conscious of being. Things will disappear only as man changes his consciousness. Deny it if you will, it still remains a fact that consciousness is the only reality and things but mirror that which you are conscious of being. The heavenly state you seek will be found only in consciousness, for the Kingdom of Heaven is within you.

Your consciousness is the only living reality, the eternal head of creation. That which you are conscious of being is the temporal body that you wear.

Neville Goddard - Consciousness: The Giver Of All Gifts

To turn your attention from that which you are aware of being is to decapitate that body; but, just as a chicken or snake continues to jump and throb for a while after its head has been removed, likewise qualities and conditions appear to live for a while after your attention has been taken from them.

Man, not knowing this law of consciousness, constantly gives thought to his previous habitual conditions and, through being attentive to them, places upon these dead bodies the eternal head of creation; thereby he reanimates and re-resurrects them.

You must leave these dead bodies alone and let the dead bury the dead. Man, having put his hand to the plough (that is, after assuming the consciousness of the quality desired), by looking back, can only defeat his fitness for the Kingdom of Heaven.

As the will of heaven is ever done on earth, you are today, in the heaven that you have established within yourself, for here on this very earth your heaven reveals itself. The Kingdom of Heaven really is at hand. Now is the accepted time.

So create a new heaven,

enter into a new state of consciousness,

and a new earth will appear.

(From Your Faith Is Your Fortune)

Neville Goddard - Consciousness: The Giver Of All Gifts

"They went forth, and entered into a ship, and that night they caught nothing."

"And He said unto them, Cast the net on the right side of the ship, and ye shall find. They cast therefore, and now they were notable to draw it for the multitude of fishes."

It is recorded that the disciples fished all night and caught nothing. Then Jesus appeared upon the scene and told them to cast their nets again, but, this time, to cast them on the right side. Peter obeyed the voice of Jesus and cast his nets once more into the waters. Where but a moment before the water was completely empty of fish, the nets almost broke with the number of the resulting catch.

Man, fishing all through the night of human ignorance, attempts to realize his desires through effort and struggle, only to find in the end that his search is fruitless.

When man discovers his awareness of being to be Christ Jesus, he will obey its voice and let it direct his fishing. He will cast his hook on the right side; he will apply the law in the right manner and will seek in consciousness for the thing desired. Finding it there, he will know that it will be multiplied in the world of form.

Those who have had the pleasure of fishing know what a thrill it is to feel the fish upon the hook. The bite of the fish is followed by the play of the fish; this play, in turn, is followed by the landing of the fish.

Something similar takes place in the consciousness of man as he fishes for the manifestations of life.

Fishermen know that if they wish to catch big fish, they must fish in deep waters; if you would catch a large measure of life, you must leave behind you the shallow waters with its many reefs and barriers and launch out into the deep blue waters where the big ones play. To catch the large manifestations of life you must enter into deeper and freer states of consciousness; only in these depths do the big expressions of life live.

Here is a simple formula for successful fishing.

First, decide what it is you want to express or possess. This is essential. You must definitely know what you want of life before you can fish for it.

After your decision is made, turn from the world of sense, remove your attention from the problem and place it on just being, by repeating quietly but with feeling,

"I AM".

As your attention is removed from the world round about you and placed upon the I AM, so that you are lost in the feeling of simply being, you will find yourself slipping the anchor that tied you to the shallows of your problem; and effortlessly you will find yourself moving out into the deep.

The sensation which accompanies this act is one of expansion. You will feel yourself rise and expand as though you were actually growing. Do not be afraid of this floating, growing experience for you are not going to die to anything but your limitations. However, your limitations are going to die as you move away from them for they live only in your consciousness.

In this deep or expanded consciousness, you will feel yourself to be a mighty pulsating power as deep and as rhythmical as the ocean. This expanded feeling is the signal that you are now in the deep blue waters where the big fish swim.

Suppose the fish you decided to catch were health and freedom; you begin to fish in this formless pulsating depth of yourself for these qualities or states of consciousness by feeling

"I AM healthy" . . "I AM free."

You continue claiming and feeling yourself to be healthy and free until the conviction that you are so possesses you. As the conviction is born within you, so that all doubts pass away and you know and feel that you are free from the limitations of the past, you will know that you have hooked these fish. The joy which courses through your entire being, on feeling that you are that which you desired to be, is equal to the thrill of the fisherman as he hooks his fish.

Now comes the play of the fish. This is accomplished by returning to the world of the senses. As you open your eyes on the world round about you, the conviction and the consciousness that you are healthy and free should be so established within you that your whole being thrills in anticipation. Then, as you walk through the necessary interval of time that it will take the things felt to embody themselves, you will feel a secret thrill in knowing that in a little while, that which no man sees, but that which you feel and know that you are, will be landed.

In a moment when you think not, while you faithfully walk in this consciousness, you will begin to express and possess that which you are conscious of being and possessing; experiencing with the fisherman the joy of landing the big one.

Now, go and fish for the manifestations of life by casting your nets in the right side.

(From Your Faith Is Your Fortune)

Neville Goddard - Consciousness: The Giver Of All Gifts

You cannot force anything outwardly by the mightiest effort of the will. There is only one way you can command the things you want and that is by assuming the consciousness of the things desired.

There is a vast difference between feeling a thing and merely knowing it intellectually.

You must accept without reservation the fact that by possessing (feeling) a thing in consciousness, you have commanded the reality that causes it to come into existence in concrete form.

You must be absolutely convinced of an unbroken connection between the invisible reality and its visible manifestation.

Your inner acceptance must become an intense, unalterable conviction which transcends both reason and intellect, renouncing entirely any belief in the reality of the externalization except as a reflection of an inner state of consciousness.

When you really understand and believe these things, you will have built up so profound a certainty that nothing can shake you.

Your desires are the invisible realities which respond only to the commands of God.

God commands the invisible to appear by claiming himself to be the thing commanded.

> *"He made Himself equal with God and found it not robbery to do the works of God."*

Now let this saying sink deep in your ear:

Be conscious of being, that which you want to appear.

(From Your Faith Is Your Fortune)

Neville Goddard - Consciousness: The Giver Of All Gifts

"Then cometh Jesus with them unto a place called Gethsemane, and saith unto the disciples, Sit ye here, while I go and pray yonder."

A most wonderful mystical romance is told in the story of Jesus in the Garden of Gethsemane, but man has failed to see the light of its symbology and has mistakenly interpreted this mystical union as an agonizing experience in which Jesus pleaded in vain with His Father to change His destiny.

Gethsemane is, to the mystic, the Garden of Creation . . the place in consciousness where man goes to realize his defined objectives.

Gethsemane is a compound word meaning to press out an oily substance: Geth, to press out, and Shemen, an oily substance.

The story of Gethsemane reveals to the mystic, in dramatic symbology, the act of creation. Just as man contains within himself an oily substance which, in the act of creation, is pressed out into a likeness of himself, so he has within himself a divine principle (his consciousness), which conditions itself as a state of consciousness and without assistance presses out or objectifies itself.

A garden is a cultivated piece of ground, a specially prepared field, where seeds of the gardener's own choice are planted and cultivated.

Gethsemane is such a garden, the place in consciousness where the mystic goes with his properly defined objectives. This garden is entered when man takes his attention from the world round about him and places it on his objectives.

Man's clarified desires are seeds containing the power and plans of self-expression and, like the seeds within man, these, too, are buried within an oily substance (a joyful, thankful attitude of mind). As man contemplates being and possessing that which he desires to be and to possess, he has begun the process of pressing out or the spiritual act of creation. These seeds are pressed out and planted when man loses himself in a wild, mad state of joy, consciously feeling and claiming himself to be that which he formerly desired to be.

Desires expressed, or pressed out, result in the passing of that particular desire. Man cannot possess a thing and still desire to possess it, at one and the same time. So, as one consciously appropriates the feeling of being the thing desired, this desire to be the thing passes . . is realized.

The receptive attitude of mind, feeling and receiving the impression of being the thing desired, is the fertile ground or womb which receives the seed (defined objective).

The seed which is pressed out of a man grows into the likeness of the man from whom it was pressed. Likewise, the mystical seed, your conscious claim that you are that which you heretofore desired to be, will grow into the likeness of you from whom and into whom it is pressed.

Yes, Gethsemane is the cultivated garden of romance where the disciplined man goes to press seeds of joy (defined desires) out of himself into his receptive attitude of mind, there to care for and nurture them, by consciously walking in the joy of being all that formerly he desired to be.

Feel with the Great Gardener the secret thrill of knowing that things and qualities not now seen, will be seen, as soon as these conscious impressions grow and ripen to maturity.

Your consciousness is Lord and Husband; the conscious state in which you dwell is wife or beloved. This state made visible is your son bearing witness of you, his father and mother, for your visible world is made in the image and likeness of the state of consciousness in which you live; your world and the fullness thereof are nothing more or less than your defined consciousness objectified.

Knowing this to be true, see to it that you choose well the mother of your children . . that conscious state in which you live, your conception of yourself. The wise man chooses his wife with great discretion. He realizes that his children must inherit the qualities of their parents and so he devotes much time and care to the selection of their mother.

The mystic knows that the conscious state in which he lives is the choice that he has made of a wife, the mother of his children, that this state must in time embody itself within his world; so he is ever select in his choice and always claims himself to be his highest ideal. He consciously defines himself as that which he desires to be.

When man realizes that the conscious state in which he lives is the choice that he has made of a mate, he will be more careful of his moods and feelings. He will not permit himself to react to suggestions of fear, lack or any undesirable impression. Such suggestions of lack could never pass the watch of the disciplined mind of the mystic, for he knows that every conscious claim must in time be expressed as a condition of his world . . of his environment.

So, he remains faithful to his beloved, his defined objective, by defining and claiming and feeling himself to be that which he desires to express. Let a man ask himself if his defined objective would be a thing of joy and beauty if it were realized.

If his answer is in the affirmative, then he may know that his choice of a bride is a princess of Israel, a daughter of Judah, for every defined objective which expresses joy when realized is a daughter of Judah, the king of praise.

Jesus took with Him into His hour of prayer His disciples, or disciplined attributes of mind, and commanded them to watch while He prayed, so that no thought or belief that would deny the realization of His desire might enter His consciousness.

Follow the example of Jesus, who, with His desires clearly defined, entered the Garden of Gethsemane (the state of joy) accompanied by His disciples (His disciplined mind) to lose Himself in a wild joy of realization.

Neville Goddard - Consciousness: The Giver Of All Gifts

The fixing of His attention on His objective was His command to His disciplined mind to watch and remain faithful to that fixation. Contemplating the joy that would be His on realizing His desire, He began the spiritual act of generation, the act of pressing out the mystical seed . . His defined desire.

In this fixation He remained, claiming and feeling Himself to be that which He (before He entered Gethsemane) desired to be, until His whole being (consciousness) was bathed in an oily sweat (joy) resembling blood (life), in short, until His whole consciousness was permeated with the living, sustained joy of being His defined objective.

As this fixation is accomplished so that the mystic knows by his feeling of joy that he has passed from his former conscious state into his present consciousness, the Passover or Crucifixion is attained.

This crucifixion or fixation of the new conscious claim is followed by the Sabbath, a time of rest. There is always an interval of time between the impression and its expression, between the conscious claim and its embodiment. This interval is called the Sabbath, the period of rest or non-effort (the day of entombment).

To walk unmoved in the consciousness of being or possessing a certain state is to keep the Sabbath.

The story of the crucifixion beautifully expresses this mystical stillness or rest. We are told that after Jesus cried out, *"It is finished!"*

He was placed in a tomb. There He remained for the entire Sabbath. When the new state or consciousness is appropriated so you feel, by this appropriation, fixed and secure in the knowledge that it is finished, then you, too, will cry out, *"It is finished!"*

and will enter the tomb or Sabbath, an interval of time in which you will walk unmoved in the conviction that your new consciousness must be resurrected (made visible).

Neville Goddard - Consciousness: The Giver Of All Gifts

Easter, the day of resurrection, falls on the first Sunday after the full moon in Aries. The mystical reason for this is simple. A defined area will not precipitate itself in the form of rain until this area reaches the point of saturation; just so the state in which you dwell will not express itself until the whole is permeated with the consciousness that it is so . . it is finished.

Your defined objective is the imaginary state, just as the equator is the imaginary line across which the sun must pass to mark the beginning of spring. This state, like the moon, has no light or life of itself; but will reflect the light of consciousness or sun,

"I AM the light of the world"

"I AM the resurrection and the life."

As Easter is determined by the full moon in Aries, so, too, is the resurrection of your conscious claim determined, by the full consciousness of your claim, by actually living as this new conception.

Most men fail to resurrect their objectives because they fail to remain faithful to their newly defined state until this fullness is attained.

If man would bear in mind the fact that there can be no Easter or day of resurrection until after the full moon, he would realize that the state into which he has consciously passed, will be expressed or resurrected only after he has remained within the state of being, his defined objective.

Until his whole self thrills with the feeling of actually being his conscious claim, in consciously living in this state of being it, and only in this way, will man ever resurrect or realize his desire.

(From Your Faith Is Your Fortune)

Neville Goddard - Consciousness: The Giver Of All Gifts

My savior is my desire..

As I want something I am looking into the eyes of my savior.

But if I continue wanting it, I deny my Jesus, my savior, for as I want I confess I am not and

"except ye believe that I AM He ye die in your sins."

I cannot have and still continue to desire what I have. I may enjoy it, but I cannot continue wanting it.

Here is the story.

This is the feast of the Passover. Something is going to change right now, something is going to passover. Man is incapable of passing over from one state of consciousness into another unless he releases from consciousness that which he now entertains, for it anchors him where he is.

You and I may go to physical feasts year after year as the sun enters the great sign of Aries, but it means nothing to the true mystical Passover.

To keep the feast of the Passover, the psychological feast, I pass from one state of consciousness into another.

I do it by releasing Barabbas, the thief and robber that robs me of that state which I could embody within my world.

The state I seek to embody is personified in the story as Jesus the Savior. If I become what I want to be then I am saved from what I was. If I do not become it, I continue to keep locked within me a thief who robs me of being that which I could be.

These stories have no reference to any persons who lived nor to any event that ever occurred upon earth. These characters are everlasting characters in the mind of every man in the world.

Neville Goddard - Consciousness: The Giver Of All Gifts

You and I perpetually keep alive either Barabbas or Jesus. You know at every moment of time who you are entertaining.

Do not condemn a crowd for clamoring that they should release Barabbas and crucify Jesus. It is not a crowd of people called Jews. They had nothing to do with it.

If we are wise, we too should clamor for the release of that state of mind that limits us from being what we want to be, that restricts us, that does not permit us to become the ideal that we seek and strive to attain in this world.

I am not saying that you are not tonight embodying Jesus. I only remind you, that if at this very moment you have an unfulfilled ambition, then you are entertaining that which denies the fulfillment of the ambition, and that which denies it is Barabbas.

To explain the mystical, psychological transformation known as the Passover, or the crossing over, you must now become identified with the ideal that you would serve, and you must remain faithful to the ideal.

If you remain faithful to it, you not only crucify it by your faithfulness, but you resurrect it unaided by a man.

As the story goes, no man could rise early enough to roll away the stone. Unaided by a man the stone was removed, and what seemingly was dead and buried was resurrected unassisted by a man.

You walk in the consciousness of being that which you want to be, no one sees it as yet, but you do not need a man to roll away the problems and the obstacles of life in order to express that which you are conscious of being.

That state has its own unique way of becoming embodied in this world, of becoming flesh that the whole world may touch it.

Now you can see the relationship between the story of Jesus and the story of Isaac and his two sons, where one transplanted the other, where one was called the Supplanter of the other.

Why do you think those who compiled the sixty odd books of our Bible made Jacob the forefather of Jesus?

They took Jacob, who was called the Supplanter, and made him father of twelve, then they took Judah or praise, the fifth son and made him the forefather of Joseph, who is supposed to have fathered in some strange way this one called Jesus.

Jesus must supplant Barabbas as Jacob must supplant and take the place of Esau.

(From The 1948 Classroom Lectures, Assumptions Harden Into Fact)

Neville Goddard - Consciousness: The Giver Of All Gifts

I do not wish to write a book of wonders, but rather to turn man's mind back to the one and only reality, that the ancient teachers worshiped as God.

All that was said of God, was in reality said of man's consciousness, so we may say,

> "That, according as it is written, He that glorify, let him glory in his own consciousness."

No man needs help to direct him in the application of this law of consciousness.

"I AM" is the self-definition of the absolute. The root out of which everything prows.

> "I AM the vine."

What is your answer to the eternal question,

> "Who am I?"

Your answer determines the part you play in the world's drama. Your answer, that is, your concept of self, need not conform to the external reality to which it relates. This great truth is revealed in the statement,

> "Let the weak say, I am strong."

Look back over the good resolutions with which many past new years are encumbered. They lived a little while and then they died. Why? Because they were severed from their root.

Assume that you are that which you want to be. Experience in imagination what you would experience in the flesh were you already that which you want to be. Remain faithful to your assumption, so that you define yourself as that which you have assumed.

Things have no life if they are severed from their roots, and our consciousness, our "I AMness," is the root of all that springs in our world.

Neville Goddard - Consciousness: The Giver Of All Gifts

"If ye believe not that I am he, ye shall die in your sins".

That is, if I do not believe that I am already that which I desire to be, then I remain as I am and die in my present concept of self.

There is no power, outside of the consciousness of man, to resurrect and make alive that which man desires to experience.

That man who is accustomed to call up at will, whatever images he pleases, will be, by virtue of the power of his imagination, master of his fate.

"I AM the resurrection, and the life: he that believeth in me, though he were dead, yet shall he live."

"Ye shall know the truth, and the truth shall make you free."

(From Out Of This World)

Neville Goddard - Consciousness: The Giver Of All Gifts

The world, and all within it, is man's conditioned consciousness objectified.

Consciousness is the cause as well as the substance of the entire world. So it is to consciousness that we must turn if we would discover the secret of creation.

Knowledge of the law of consciousness and the method of operating this law will enable you to accomplish all you desire in life. Armed with a working knowledge of this law, you can build and maintain an ideal world.

Consciousness is the one and only reality, not figuratively but actually.

This reality may for the sake of clarity be likened unto a stream which is divided into two parts, the conscious and the subconscious. In order to intelligently operate the law of consciousness, it is necessary to understand the relationship between the conscious and the subconscious. The conscious is personal and selective; the subconscious is impersonal and non-selective. The conscious is the realm of effect; the subconscious is the realm of cause.

These two aspects are the male and female divisions of consciousness. The conscious is male; the subconscious is female.

The conscious generates ideas and impresses these ideas on the subconscious; the subconscious receives ideas and gives form and expression to them.

By this law . . first conceiving an idea and then impressing the idea conceived on the subconscious . . all things evolve out of consciousness; and without this sequence, there is not anything made that is made. The conscious impresses the subconscious, while the subconscious expresses all that is impressed upon it.

(From Feeling Is The Secret)

Neville Goddard - Consciousness: The Giver Of All Gifts

"The husband is head of the wife,"

may not be true of man and woman in their earthly relationship but it is true of the conscious and the subconscious, or the male and female aspects of consciousness.

The mystery to which Paul referred when he wrote,

"This is a great mystery...
He that loveth his wife loveth himself... .
And they two shall be one flesh,"

is simply the mystery of consciousness.

Consciousness is really one and undivided but for creation's sake it appears to be divided into two.

The conscious (objective) or male aspect truly is the head and dominates the subconscious (subjective) or female aspect. However, this leadership is not that of the tyrant, but of the lover. So, by assuming the feeling that would be yours were you already in possession of your objective, the subconscious is moved to build the exact likeness of your assumption.

Your desires are not subconsciously accepted until you assume the feeling of their reality, for only through feeling is an idea subconsciously accepted and only through this subconscious acceptance is it ever expressed.

It is easier to ascribe your feeling to events in the world than to admit that the conditions of the world reflect your feeling. However, it is eternally true that the outside mirrors the inside.

"As within so without."

"A man can receive nothing unless
it is given him from heaven,"

and

Neville Goddard - Consciousness: The Giver Of All Gifts

"The kingdom of heaven is within you."

Nothing comes from without; all things come from within . . from the subconscious.

It is impossible for you to see other than the contents of your consciousness. Your world in its every detail is your consciousness objectified. Objective states bear witness of subconscious impressions. A change of impression results in a change of expression.

The subconscious accepts as true that which you feel as true, and because creation is the result of subconscious impressions, you, by your feeling, determine creation. You are already that which you want to be, and your refusal to believe this is the only reason you do not see it.

To seek on the outside for that which you do not feel you are, is to seek in vain, for we never find that which we want; we find only that which we are.

In short, you express and have only that which you are conscious of being or possessing.

"To him that hath it is given."

Denying the evidence of the senses and appropriating the feeling of the wish fulfilled is the way to the realization of your desire.

Mastery of self-control of your thoughts and feelings is your highest achievement.

However, until perfect self-control is attained, so that, in spite of appearances, you feel all that you want to feel, use sleep and prayer to aid you in realizing your desired states.

These are the two gateways into the subconscious.

(From Feeling Is The Secret)

Neville Goddard - Consciousness: The Giver Of All Gifts

"As in heaven, so on earth."

As in the subconscious, so on earth. Whatever you have in consciousness as you go to sleep is the measure of your expression in the waking two-thirds of your life on earth. Nothing stops you from realizing your objective save your failure to feel that you are already that which you wish to be, or that you are already in possession of the thing sought.

Your subconscious gives form to your desires only when you feel your wish fulfilled.

The unconsciousness of sleep is the normal state of the subconscious. Because all things come from within yourself, and your conception of yourself determines that which comes, you should always feel the wish fulfilled before you drop off to sleep. You never draw out of the deep of yourself that which you want; you always draw that which you are, and you are that which you feel yourself to be as well as that which you feel as true of others.

To be realized, then, the wish must be resolved into the feeling of being or having or witnessing the state sought. This is accomplished by assuming the feeling of the wish fulfilled. The feeling which comes in response to the question

"How would I feel were my wish realized?"

is the feeling which should monopolize and immobilize your attention as you relax into sleep. You must be in the consciousness of being or having that which you want to be or to have before you drop off to sleep.

Once asleep, man has no freedom of choice. His entire slumber is dominated by his last waking concept of self. It follows, therefore, that he should always assume the feeling of accomplishment and satisfaction before he retires in sleep,

"Come before me with singing and thanksgiving,"

"Enter into his gates with thanksgiving and into his courts with praise."

Neville Goddard - Consciousness: The Giver Of All Gifts

Your mood prior to sleep defines your state of consciousness as you enter into the presence of your everlasting lover, the subconscious. She sees you exactly as you feel yourself to be. If, as you prepare for sleep, you assume and maintain the consciousness of success by feeling

"I AM successful",

you must be successful.

(From Feeling Is The Secret)

It is only by a change of consciousness, by actually changing your concept of yourself, that you can

"build more stately mansions",

the manifestations of higher and higher concepts. By manifesting is meant experiencing the results of these concepts in your world.

It is of vital importance to understand clearly just what consciousness is.

The reason lies in the fact that consciousness is the one and only reality, it is the first and only cause-substance of the phenomena of life.

Nothing has existence for man save through the consciousness he has of it. Therefore, it is to consciousness you must turn, for it is the only foundation on which the phenomena of life can be explained.

If we accept the idea of a first cause, it would follow that the evolution of that cause could never result in anything foreign to itself.

That is, if the first cause-substance is light, all its evolutions, fruits and manifestations would remain light.

The first cause-substance being consciousness, all its evolutions, fruits and phenomena must remain consciousness. All that could be observed would be a higher or lower form or variation of the same thing. In other words, if your consciousness is the only reality, it must also be the only substance.

Consequently, what appears to you as circumstances, conditions and even material objects is really only the product of your own consciousness.

Nature, then, as a thing or a complex of things external to your mind, must be rejected. You and your environment cannot be regarded as existing separately.

Neville Goddard - Consciousness: The Giver Of All Gifts

You and your world are one.

Therefore, you must turn from the objective appearance of things to the subjective center of things, your consciousness, if you truly desire to know the cause of the phenomena of life, and how to use this knowledge to realize your fondest dreams.

In the midst of the apparent contradictions, antagonisms and contrasts of your life, there is only one principle at work, only your consciousness operating.

Difference does not consist in variety of substance, but in variety of arrangement of the same cause-substance, your consciousness.

The world moves with motiveless necessity. By this is meant that it has no motive of its own, but is under the necessity of manifesting your concept, the arrangement of your mind, and your mind is always arranged in the image of all you believe and consent to as true.

The rich man, poor man, beggar man or thief are not different minds, but different arrangements of the same mind, in the same sense that a piece of steel, when magnetized, differs not in substance from its demagnetized state, but in the arrangement and order of its molecules.

A single electron revolving in a specified orbit constitutes the unit of magnetism. When a piece of steel or anything else is demagnetized, the revolving electrons have not stopped. Therefore, the magnetism has not gone out of existence. There is only a rearrangement of the particles, so that they produce no outside or perceptible effect.

When particles are arranged at random, mixed up in all directions, the substance is said to be demagnetized; but when particles are marshaled in ranks so that a number of them face in one direction, the substance is a magnet.

Magnetism is not generated; it is displayed.

Health, wealth, beauty and genius are not created; they are only manifested by the arrangement of your mind, that is, by your concept of yourself, and your concept of yourself is all that you accept and consent to as true. What you consent to can only be discovered by an uncritical observation of your reactions to life.

Your reactions reveal where you live psychologically; and where you live psychologically determines how you live here in the outer visible world.

The importance of this in your daily life should be immediately apparent. The basic nature of the primal cause is consciousness.

Therefore, the ultimate substance of all things is consciousness.

(From The Power of Awareness)

Neville Goddard - Consciousness: The Giver Of All Gifts

Man's chief delusion is his conviction that there are causes other than his own state of consciousness.

All that befalls a man, all that is done by him, all that comes from him, happens as a result of his state of consciousness.

A man's consciousness is all that he thinks and desires and loves, all that he believes is true and consents to.

That is why a change of consciousness is necessary before you can change your outer world.

(From The Power of Awareness)

Neville Goddard - Consciousness: The Giver Of All Gifts

The changes which take place in your life as a result of your changed concept of yourself always appear to the unenlightened to be the result, not of a change of your consciousness, but of chance, outer cause, or coincidence.

However, the only fate governing your life is the fate determined by your own concepts, your own assumptions; for an assumption, though false, if persisted in, will harden into fact.

The ideal you seek and hope to attain will not manifest itself, will not be realized by you until you have imagined that you are already that ideal.

There is no escape for you except by a radical psychological transformation of yourself, except by your assumption of the feeling of your wish fulfilled. Therefore, make results or accomplishments the crucial test of your ability to use your imagination.

Everything depends on your attitude towards yourself. That which you will not affirm as true of yourself can never be realized by you, for that attitude alone is the necessary condition by which you realize your goal.

All transformation is based upon suggestion, and this can work only where you lay yourself completely open to an influence.

You must abandon yourself to your ideal as a woman abandons herself to love, for complete abandonment of self to it is the way to union with your ideal.

You must assume the feeling of the wish fulfilled until your assumption has all the sensory vividness of reality. You must imagine that you are already experiencing what you desire. That is, you must assume the feeling of the fulfillment of your desire until you are possessed by it and this feeling crowds all other ideas out of your consciousness.

(From The Power of Awareness)

Now is the time to control your imagination and

*"Give beauty for ashes, joy for mourning,
praise for the spirit of heaviness, that they
might be called trees of righteousness, the
planting of the Lord that He might be glorified."*

You give beauty for ashes when you concentrate your attention on things as you would like them to be rather than on things as they are.

You give joy for mourning when you maintain a joyous attitude regardless of unfavorable circumstances.

You give praise for the spirit of heaviness when you maintain a confident attitude instead of succumbing to despondency.

In this quotation, the Bible uses the word tree as a synonym for man. You become a tree of righteousness when the above mental states are a permanent part of your consciousness. You are a planting of the Lord when all your thoughts are true thoughts.

(From The Power of Awareness)

Neville Goddard - Consciousness: The Giver Of All Gifts

Your destiny is that which you must inevitably experience.

Really it is an infinite number of individual destinies, each of which when attained is the starting place for a new destiny.

Since life is infinite, the concept of an ultimate destiny is inconceivable.

When we understand that consciousness is the only reality, we know that it is the only creator. This means that your consciousness is the creator of your destiny.

The fact is, you are creating your destiny every moment, whether you know it or not. Much that is good and even wonderful has come into your life without your having any inkling that you were the creator of it.

However, the understanding of the causes of your experience, and the knowledge that you are the sole creator of the contents of your life, both good and bad, not only make you a much keener observer of all phenomena, but through the awareness of the power of your own consciousness, intensify your appreciation of the richness and grandeur of life.

Regardless of occasional experiences to the contrary, it is your destiny to rise to higher and higher states of consciousness, and to bring into manifestation more and more of creation's infinite wonders.

Actually, you are destined to reach the point where you realize that, through your own desire, you can consciously create your successive destinies.

(From The Power of Awareness)

Neville Goddard - Consciousness: The Giver Of All Gifts

No help cometh from without; the hills to which we lift our eyes are those of an inner range.

It is thus to our own consciousness that we must turn as to the only reality, the only foundation on which all phenomena can be explained. We can rely absolutely on the justice of this law to give us only that which is of the nature of ourselves.

To attempt to change the world before we change our concept of ourselves is to struggle against the nature of things. There can be no outer change until there is first an inner change.

As within, so without.

I am not advocating philosophical indifference when I suggest that we should imagine ourselves as already that which we want to be, living in a mental atmosphere of greatness, rather than using physical means and arguments to bring about the desired change.

Everything we do, unaccompanied by a change of consciousness, is but futile readjustment of surfaces. However we toil or struggle, we can receive no more than our subconscious assumptions affirm.

To protest against anything which happens to us is to protest against the law of our being and our rulership over our own destiny.

The circumstances of my life are too closely related to my conception of myself not to have been launched by my own spirit from some magical storehouse of my being. If there is pain to me in these happenings, I should look within myself for the cause, for I am moved here and there and made to live in a world in harmony with my concept of myself.

Intense meditation brings about a union with the state contemplated, and during this union we see visions, have experiences, and behave in keeping with our change of consciousness.

Neville Goddard - Consciousness: The Giver Of All Gifts

This shows us that a transformation of consciousness will result in a change of environment and behavior.

However, our ordinary alterations of consciousness, as we pass from one state to another, are not transformations, because each of them is so rapidly succeeded by another in the reverse direction; but whenever one state grows so stable as to definitely expel its rivals, then that central habitual state defines the character and is a true transformation. To say that we are transformed means that ideas previously peripheral in our consciousness now take a central place and form the habitual center of our energy.

All wars prove that violent emotions are extremely potent in precipitating mental rearrangements. Every great conflict has been followed by an era of materialism and greed in which the ideals for which the conflict ostensibly was waged are submerged. This is inevitable because war evokes hate, which impels a descent in consciousness from the plane of the ideal to the level where the conflict is waged.

If we would become as emotionally aroused over our ideals as we become over our dislikes, we would ascend to the plane of our ideals as easily as we now descend to the level of our hates.

Love and hate have a magical transforming power, and we grow through their exercise into the likeness of what we contemplate. By intensity of hatred we create in ourselves the character we imagine in our enemies.

Qualities die for want of attention, so the unlovely states might best be rubbed out by imagining "beauty for ashes and joy for mourning" rather than by direct attacks on the state from which we would be free.

(From Awakened Imagination And The Search)

Neville Goddard - Consciousness: The Giver Of All Gifts

Whatever you desire is already

"furnished and prepared".

Your imagination can put you in touch inwardly with that state of consciousness. If you imagine that you are already the one you want to be,

you are following the

"man bearing a pitcher of water".

If you remain in that state, you have entered the guest-chamber . . Passover . . and committed your spirit into the hands of God . . your consciousness.

A man's state of consciousness is his demand on the Infinite Store House of God, and, like the law of commerce, a demand creates a supply.

To change the supply, you change the demand . . your state of consciousness.

What you desire to be, that you must feel you already are. Your state of consciousness creates the conditions of your life, rather than the conditions create your state of consciousness.

To know this Truth, is to have the

"water of life".

But your savior . . the solution of your problem . . cannot be manifested by such knowledge only.

It can be realized only as such knowledge is applied.

Only as you assume the feeling of your wish fulfilled, and continue therein, is your side pierced;

"from whence cometh blood and water".

In this manner only is Jesus, the solution of your problem, realized.

> "for thou must know that in the government of the mind thou art thine own lord and master, that there will rise up no fire in the circle or whole circumference of thy body and spirit, unless thou awakes it thyself."
> . . . Jacob Boehme

God is your consciousness.

His promises are conditional. Unless the demand, your state of consciousness, is changed, the supply . . the present conditions of your life, remain as they are.

"As we forgive"

as we change our mind, the law is automatic. Your state of consciousness is the spring of action, the directing force, and that which creates the supply.

(From Seedtime And Harvest)

Neville Goddard - Consciousness: The Giver Of All Gifts

HEAR, O Israel: the Lord our God is one Lord.
Hear, O Israel:

Hear, O man made of the very substance of God: You and God are one and undivided! Man, the world and all within it are conditioned states of the unconditioned one, God. You are this one; you are God conditioned as man. All that you believe God to be, you are; but you will never know this to be true until you stop claiming it of another, and recognize this seeming other to be yourself.

God and man, spirit and matter, the formless and the formed, the creator and the creation, the cause and the effect, your Father and you are one.

This one, in whom all conditioned states live and move and have their being, is your I AM, your unconditioned consciousness.

> Unconditioned consciousness is God, the one and only reality.

By unconditioned consciousness is meant a sense of awareness; a sense of knowing that I AM apart from knowing who I AM; the consciousness of being, divorced from that which I am conscious of being. I AM aware of being man, but I need not be man to be aware of being.

Before I became aware of being someone, I, unconditioned awareness, was aware of being, and this awareness does not depend upon being someone. I AM self-existent, unconditioned consciousness; I became aware of being someone; and I shall become aware of being someone other than this that I am now aware of being; but I AM eternally aware of being whether I AM unconditioned formlessness or I AM conditioned form.

As the conditioned state, I (man), might forget who I am, or where I am, but I cannot forget that I AM.

This knowing that I AM, this awareness of being, is the only reality.

Neville Goddard - Consciousness: The Giver Of All Gifts

This unconditioned consciousness, the I AM, is that knowing reality in whom all conditioned states . . conceptions of myself . . begin and end, but which ever remains the unknown knowing being when all the known ceases to be.

All that I have ever believed myself to be, all that I now believe myself to be, and all that I shall ever believe myself to be, are but attempts to know myself . . the unknown, undefined reality.

This unknown knowing one, or unconditioned consciousness, is my true being, the one and only reality. I AM the unconditioned reality conditioned as that which I believe myself to be.

I AM the believer limited by my beliefs, the knower defined by the known.

The world is my conditioned consciousness objectified. That which I feel and believe to be true of myself is now projected in space as my world. The world, my mirrored self, ever bears witness of the state of consciousness in which I live.

There is no chance or accident responsible for the things that happen to me or the environment in which I find myself. Nor is predestined fate the author of my fortunes or misfortunes. Innocence and guilt are mere words with no meaning to the law of consciousness, except as they reflect the state of consciousness itself.

The consciousness of guilt calls forth condemnation. The consciousness of lack produces poverty. Man everlastingly objectifies the state of consciousness in which he abides but he has somehow or other become confused in the interpretation of the law of cause and effect.

He has forgotten that it is the inner state which is the cause of the outer manifestation . .

(From Freedom For All)

"As within, so without"

and in his forgetfulness he believes that an outside God has his own peculiar reason for doing things, such reasons being beyond the comprehension of mere man; or he believes that people are suffering because of past mistakes which have been forgotten by the conscious mind; or, again, that blind chance alone plays the part of God.

One day man will realize that his own I AM-ness is the God he has been seeking throughout the ages, and that his own sense of awareness . . his consciousness of being . . is the one and only reality.

The most difficult thing for man to really grasp is this:

That the "I AM-ness" in himself is God. It is his true being or Father state, the only state he can be sure of. The Son, his conception of himself, is an illusion.

He always knows that he is, but that which he is, is an illusion created by himself (the Father) in an attempt at self-definition.

This discovery reveals that all that I have believed God to be, I AM.

"I AM the resurrection and the life"

is a statement of fact concerning my consciousness, for my consciousness resurrects or makes visibly alive that which I AM conscious of being.

"I AM the door ... all that ever came before me are thieves and robbers"

shows me that my consciousness is the one and only entrance into the world of expression; that by assuming the consciousness of being or possessing the thing which I desire to be or possess is the only way by which I can become it or possess it; that any attempt to express this desirable state in ways other than by assuming the consciousness of being or possessing it, is to be robbed of the joy of expression and possession.

"I AM the beginning and the end"

reveals my consciousness as the cause of the birth and death of all expression.

"I AM hath sent me"

reveals my consciousness to be the Lord which sends me into the world in the image and likeness of that which I am conscious of being to live in a world composed of all that I am conscious of.

"I AM the Lord, and there is no God beside me,"

declares my consciousness to be the one and only Lord and beside my consciousness there is no God.

"Be still and know that I AM God"

means that I should still the mind and know that consciousness is God.

"Thou shalt not take the Name of the Lord thy God in vain."

"I AM the Lord: that is My Name."

Now that you have discovered your I AM, your consciousness to be God, do not claim anything to be true of yourself that you would not claim to be true of God, for in defining yourself, you are defining God.

That which you are conscious of being is that which you have named God. God and man are one. You and your Father are one.

Your unconditioned consciousness, or I AM, and that which you are conscious of being, are one. The conceiver and the conception are one.

Neville Goddard - Consciousness: The Giver Of All Gifts

If your conception of yourself is less than that which you claim as true of God, you have robbed God, the Father, because you (the Son or conception) bear witness of the Father or conceiver.

Do not take the magical Name of God, I AM, in vain for you will not be held guiltless; you must express all that you claim yourself to be. Name God by consciously defining yourself as your highest ideal.

(From Freedom For All)

It cannot be stated too often that consciousness is the one and only reality, for this is the truth that sets man free.

This is the foundation upon which the whole structure of biblical literature rests. The stories of the Bible are all mystical revelations written in an Eastern symbolism which reveals to the intuitive the secret of creation and the formula of escape.

The Bible is man's attempt to express in words the cause and manner of creation.

Man discovered that his consciousness was the cause or creator of his world, so he proceeded to tell the story of creation in a series of symbolical stories known to us today as the Bible.

To understand this greatest of books you need a little intelligence and much intuition . . intelligence enough to enable you to read the book, and intuition enough to interpret and understand what you read.

You may ask why the Bible was written symbolically. Why was it not written in a clear, simple style so that all who read it might understand it? To these questions I reply that all men speak symbolically to that part of the world which differs from their own.

The language of the West is clear to us of the West, but it is symbolic to the East; and vice versa. An example of this can be found in the Easterner's instruction:

> "If thine hand offend thee, cut it off."

He speaks of the hand, not as the hand of the body, but as any form of expression, and thereby he warns you to turn from that expression in your world which is offensive to you.

At the same time the man of the West would unintentionally mislead the man of the East by saying:

Neville Goddard - Consciousness: The Giver Of All Gifts

"This bank is on the rocks."

For the expression

"on the rocks"

to the Westerner is equivalent to bankruptcy while a rock to an Easterner is a symbol of faith and security.

"I will like him unto a wise man which built his house upon a rock; and the rain descended, and the floods came, and the winds blew and beat upon that house; and it fell not; for it was founded upon a rock."

To really understand the message of the Bible you must bear in mind that it was written by the Eastern mind and therefore cannot be taken literally by those of the West.

Biologically, there is no difference between the East and the West. Love and hate are the same; hunger and thirst are the same; ambition and desire are the same; but the technique of expression is vastly different.

The first thing you must discover if you would unlock the secret of the Bible, is the meaning of the symbolic name of the creator which is known to all as Jehovah.

This word "Jehovah" is composed of the four Hebrew letters . . JOD HE VAU HE. The whole secret of creation is concealed within this name.

The first letter, JOD, represents the absolute state or consciousness unconditioned; the sense of undefined awareness; that all-inclusiveness out of which all creation or conditioned states of consciousness come. In the terminology of today JOD is I AM, or unconditioned consciousness.

The second letter, HE, represents the only begotten Son, a desire, an imaginary state. It symbolizes an idea; a defined subjective state or clarified mental picture.

The third letter, VAU, symbolizes the act of unifying or joining the conceiver (JOD), the consciousness desiring to the conception (HE), the state desired, so that the conceiver and the conception become one. Fixing a mental state, consciously defining yourself as the state desired, impressing upon yourself the fact that you are now that which you imagined or conceived as your objective, is the function of VAU.

It nails or joins the consciousness desiring to the thing desired. The cementing or joining process is accomplished subjectively by feeling the reality of that which is not yet objectified.

The fourth letter, HE, represents the objectifying of this subjective agreement. The JOD HE VAU makes man or the manifested world (HE), in the image and likeness of itself, the subjective conscious state. So the function of the final HE is to objectively bear witness to the subjective state JOD HE VAU. Conditioned consciousness continually objectifies itself on the screen of space. The world is the image and likeness of the subjective conscious state which created it. The visible world of itself can do nothing; it only bears record of its creator, the subjective state. It is the visible Son (HE) bearing witness of the invisible Father, Son and Mother . . JOD HE VAU . . a Holy Trinity which can only be seen when made visible as man or manifestation.

Your unconditioned consciousness (JOD) is your I AM which visualizes or imagines a desirable state (HE), and then becomes conscious of being that state imagined by feeling and believing itself to be the imagined state. The conscious union between you who desire and that which you desire to be, is made possible through the VAU, or your capacity to feel and believe.

Believing is simply living in the feeling of actually being the state imagined, by assuming the consciousness of being the state desired. The subjective state symbolized as JOD HE VAU then objectifies itself as HE, thereby completing the mystery of the creator's name and nature, JOD HE VAU HE (Jehovah). JOD is to be aware; HE is to be aware of something; VAU is to be aware as, or to be aware of being that which you were only aware of. The second HE is your visible objectified world which is made in the image and likeness of the JOD HE VAU, or that which you are aware of being.

> *"And God said, Let Us make man in
> Our image, after Our likeness."*

Let us, JOD HE VAU make the objective manifestation (HE) in our image, the image of the subjective state. The world is the objectified likeness of the subjective conscious state in which consciousness abides.

This understanding that consciousness is the one and only reality is the foundation of the Bible.

The stories of the Bible are attempts to reveal in symbolic language the secret of creation as well as to show man the one formula to escape from all of his own creations.

This is the true meaning of the name of Jehovah, the name by which all things are made and without which there is nothing made that is made.

First, you are aware; then you become aware of something; then you become aware as that which you were aware of; then you behold objectively that which you are aware of being.

(From Freedom For All)

Neville Goddard - Consciousness: The Giver Of All Gifts

Let us take one of the stories of the Bible and see how the prophets and writers of old revealed the story of creation by this strange Eastern symbolism.

We all know the story of Noah and the Ark; that Noah was chosen to create a new world after the world was destroyed by the flood.

The Bible tells us that Noah had three sons, Shem, Ham and Japheth.

The first son is called Shem, which means name. Ham. The second son, means warm, alive. The third son is called Japheth, which means extension.

You will observe that Noah and his three sons Shem, Ham and Japheth contain the same formula of creation as does the divine name of JOD HE VAU HE.

Noah, the Father, the conceiver, the builder of a new world is equivalent to the JOD, or unconditioned consciousness, I AM.

Shem is your desire; that which you are conscious of; that which you name and define as your objective, and is equivalent to the second letter in the divine name (HE).

Ham is the warm, live state of feeling, which joins or binds together consciousness desiring and the thing desired, and is therefore equivalent to the third letter in the divine name, the VAU.

The last son, Japheth, means extension, and is the extended or objectified state bearing witness of the subjective state and is equivalent to the last letter in the divine name, HE.

You are Noah, the knower, the creator. The first thing you beget is an idea, an urge, a desire, the word, or your first son Shem (name).

Your second son Ham (warm, alive) is the secret of feeling by which you are joined to your desire subjectively so that you, the consciousness desiring, become conscious of being or possessing the thing desired.

Your third son, Japheth, is the confirmation, the visible proof that you know the secret of creation. He is the extended or objectified state bearing witness of the invisible or subjective state in which you abide.

In the story of Noah it is recorded that Ham saw the secrets of his Father, and because of his discovery, he was made to serve his brothers, Shem and Japheth.

Ham, or feeling, is the secret of the Father, your I AM, for it is through feeling that the consciousness desiring is joined to the thing desired. The conscious union or mystical marriage is made possible only through feeling. It is feeling which performs this heavenly union of Father and Son,

Noah and Shem, unconditioned consciousness and conditioned consciousness. By performing this service, feeling automatically serves Japheth, the extended or expressed state, for there can be no objectified expression unless there is first a subjective impression.

To feel the presence of the thing desired, to subjectively actualize a state by impressing upon yourself, through feeling, a definite conscious state is the secret of creation.

Your present objectified world is Japheth which was made visible by Ham. Therefore Ham serves his brothers Shem and Japheth, for without feeling which is symbolized as Ham, the idea or thing desired (Shem) could not be made visible as Japheth.

The ability to feel the unseen, the ability to actualize and make real a definite subjective state through the sense of feeling is the secret of creation, the secret by which the word or unseen desire is made visible . . is made flesh.

> *"And God calleth things that be
> not as though they were."*

Consciousness calls things that are not seen as though they were, and it does this by first defining itself as that which it desires to express, and second by remaining within the defined state until the invisible becomes visible. Here is the perfect working of the law according to the story of Noah. This very moment you are aware of being.

This awareness of being, this knowing that you are, is Noah, the creator.

Now with Noah's identity established as your own consciousness of being, name something that you would like to possess or express; define some objective (Shem), and with your desire clearly defined, close your eyes and feel that you have it or are expressing it.

Don't question how it can be done; simply feel that you have it. Assume the attitude of mind that would be yours if you were already in possession of it so that you feel that it is done.

Feeling is the secret of creation.

Be as wise as Ham and make this discovery that you too may have the joy of serving your brothers Shem and Japheth; the joy of making the word or name flesh.

(From Freedom For All)

THE SECRET OF FEELING
(Complete Chapter From Freedom For All)

The secret of feeling or the calling of the invisible into visible states is beautifully told in the story of Isaac blessing his second son Jacob by the belief, based solely upon feeling, that he was blessing his first son Esau.

It is recorded that Isaac, who was old and blind, felt that he was about to leave this world and wishing to bless his first son Esau before he died, sent Esau hunting for savory venison with the promise that upon his return from the hunt he would receive his father's blessing.

Now Jacob, who desired the birthright or right to be born through the blessing of his father, overheard his blind father's request for venison and his promise to Esau. So, as Esau went hunting for the venison, Jacob killed and dressed a kid of his father's flock.

Placing the skins upon his smooth body to give him the feel of his hairy and rough brother Esau, he brought the tastily prepared kid to his blind father Isaac. And Isaac who depended solely upon his sense of feel mistook his second son Jacob for his first son Esau, and pronounced his blessing on Jacob.

Esau on his return from the hunt learned that his smooth-skinned brother Jacob had supplanted him so he appealed to his father for justice; but Isaac answered and said,

"Thy brother came with subtlety and hath taken away thy blessing.

I have made him thy Lord, and all his brethren have I given to him for servants."

Simple human decency should tell man that this story cannot be taken literally.

There must be a message for man hidden somewhere in this treacherous and despicable act of Jacob!

The hidden message, the formula of success buried in this story was intuitively revealed to the writer in this manner:

Isaac, the blind father, is your consciousness; your awareness of being.

Esau, the hairy son, is your present objectified world . . the rough or sensibly felt; the present moment; the present environment; your present conception of yourself; in short, the world you know by reason of your objective senses.

Jacob, the smooth-skinned lad, the second son, is your desire or subjective state, an idea not yet embodied, a subjective state which is perceived and sensed but not objectively known or seen; a point in time and space removed from the present. In short, Jacob is your defined objective.

The smooth-skinned Jacob . . or subjective state seeking embodiment or the right of birth . . when properly felt or blessed by his father (when consciously felt and fixed as real), becomes objectified; and in so doing he supplants the rough, hairy Esau, or the former objectified state.

Two things cannot occupy a given place at one and the same time, and so as the invisible is made visible, the former visible state vanishes.

Your consciousness is the cause of your world. The conscious state in which you abide determines the kind of world in which you live.

Your present concept of yourself is now objectified as your environment, and this state is symbolized as Esau, the hairy, or sensibly felt; the first son.

That which you would like to be or possess is symbolized as your second son, Jacob, the smooth-skinned lad who is not yet seen but is subjectively senses and felt, and will, if properly touched, supplant his brother Esau, or your present world.

Neville Goddard - Consciousness: The Giver Of All Gifts

Always bear in mind the fact that Isaac, the father of these two sons, or states, is blind. He does not see his smooth-skinned son Jacob; he only feels him. And through the sense of feeling he actually believes Jacob, the subjective, to be Esau, the real, the objectified.

You do not see your desire objectively; you simply sense it (feel it) subjectively. You do not grope in space after a desirable state.

Like Isaac, you sit still and send your first son hunting by removing your attention from your objective world. Then in the absence of your first son, Esau, you invite the desirable state, your second son, Jacob, to come close so that you may feel it.

> *"Come close, my son, that I may feel you."*

First, you are aware of it in your immediate environment; then you draw it closer and closer and closer until you sense it and feel it in your immediate presence so that it is real and natural to you.

> *"If two of you shall agree on earth as touching on any point that they shall ask, it shall be done for them of My Father, Which is in heaven."*

The two agree, through the sense of feel, and the agreement is established on earth .. is objectified, is made real.

The two agreeing are Isaac and Jacob .. you and that which you desire; and the agreement is made solely on the sense of feeling.

Esau symbolizes your present objectified world whether it be pleasant or otherwise.

Jacob symbolizes any and every desire of your heart.

Isaac symbolizes your true self .. with your eyes closed to the present world .. in the act of sensing and feeling yourself to be or to possess that which you desire to be or to possess.

Neville Goddard - Consciousness: The Giver Of All Gifts

The secret of Isaac, the sensing, feeling state, is simply the act of mentally separating the sensibly felt (your present physical state) from the insensibly felt (that which you would like to be).

With the objective senses tightly shut, Isaac made, and you can make, the insensibly felt, (the subjective state), seem real or sensibly known, for faith is knowledge.

Knowing the law of self-expression, the law by which the invisible is made visible, is not enough. *It must be applied*; and this is the method of application.

First: Send your first son Esau . . your present objectified world or problem . . hunting. This is accomplished simply by closing your eyes and taking your attention away from the objectified limitations. As your senses are removed from your objective world, it vanishes from your consciousness or goes hunting.

Second: With your eyes still closed and your attention removed from the world round about you, consciously fix the natural time and place for the realization of your desire.

With your objective senses closed to your present environment, you can sense and feel the reality of any point in time or space, for both are psychological and can be created at will.

It is vitally important that the natural time-space condition of Jacob, that is, the natural time and place for the realization of your desire, be first fixed in your consciousness.

If Sunday is the day on which the thing desired is to be realized, then Sunday must be fixed in consciousness now. Simply begin to feel that it is Sunday until the quietness and naturalness of Sunday is consciously established. You have definite associations with the days, weeks, months and seasons of the year. You have said time and again "Today feels like Sunday, or Monday, or Saturday; or this feels like Spring, or summer, or Fall, or Winter."

Neville Goddard - Consciousness: The Giver Of All Gifts

This should convince you that you have definite, conscious impressions that you associate with the days, weeks, and seasons of the year. Then because of these associations you can select any desirable time, and by recalling the conscious impression associated with such time, you can make a subjective reality of that time, now.

Do the same with space. If the room in which you are seated is not the room in which the thing desired would be naturally placed or realized, feel yourself seated in the room or place where it would be natural. Consciously fix this time space impression before you start the act of sensing and feeling the nearness, the reality, and the possession of the thing desired. It matters not whether the place desired be ten thousand miles away or only next door, you must fix in consciousness the fact that right where you are seated, is the desired place.

You do not make a mental journey; you collapse space. Sit quietly where you are, and make "thereness" . . "hereness." Close your eyes and feel that the very place where you are, is the place desired; feel and sense the reality of it until you are consciously impressed with this fact, for your knowledge of this fact is based solely on your subjective sensing.

Third: In the absence of Esau (the problem) and with the natural time-space established, you invite Jacob (the solution), to come and fill this space . . to come and supplant his brother.

In your imagination, see the thing desired. If you cannot visualize it, sense the general outline of it; contemplate it. Then mentally draw it close to you.

"Come close, my son, that I may feel you."

Feel the nearness of it; feel it to be in your immediate presence; feel the reality and solidity of it; feel it and see it naturally placed in the room in which you are seated; feel the thrill of actual accomplishment, and the joy of possession.

Now open your eyes.

This brings you back to the objective world . . the rough or sensibly felt world.

Your hairy son Esau has returned from the hunt and by his very presence tells you that you have been betrayed by your smooth-skinned son Jacob . . the subjective, psychologically felt. But, like Isaac, whose confidence was based upon the knowledge of this changeless law, you too will say,

> *"I have made him thy Lord and all his brethren have I given to him for servants".*

That is, even though your problems appears fixed and real, you have felt the subjective, psychological state to be real to the point of receiving the thrill of that reality; you have experienced the secret of creation, for you have felt the reality of the subjective.

You have fixed a definite psychological state which in spite of all opposition or precedent will objectify itself, thereby fulfilling the name of Jacob . . the supplanter.

Here are a few practical examples of this drama.

First: The blessing or making a thing real.

Sit in your living room and name a piece of furniture, rug or lamp that you would like to have in this particular room. Look at that area of the room where you would place it if you had it. Close your eyes and let all that now occupies that area of the room vanish.

In your imagination see this area as empty space . . there is absolutely nothing there. Now begin to fill this space with the desired piece of furniture; sense and feel that you have it in this very area, imagine you are seeing that which you desired to see. Continue in this consciousness until you feel the thrill of possession.

Second. The blessing or the making of a place real.

You are now seated in your apartment in New York City, contemplating the joy that would be yours if you were on an ocean liner sailing across the great Atlantic.

> *"I go to prepare a place for you. And if I go and prepare a place for you, I will come again, and receive you unto myself; that where I am there ye may be also."*

Your eyes are closed; you have consciously released the New York apartment and in its place you sense and feel that you are on an ocean liner. You are seated in a deck chair; there is nothing round you but the vast Atlantic.

Fix the reality of this ship and ocean so that in this state you can mentally recall the day when you were seated in your New York apartment dreaming of this day at sea. Recall the mental picture of yourself seated there in New York dreaming of this day. In your imagination see the memory picture of yourself back there in your New York apartment.

If you succeed in looking back on your New York apartment without consciously returning there, then you have successfully prepared the reality of this voyage.

Remain in this conscious state feeling the reality of the ship and the ocean; feel the joy of this accomplishment . . then open your eyes. You have gone and prepared the place; you have fixed a definite psychological state and where you are in consciousness there you shall be in body also.

Third: The blessing or making real of a point in time.

You consciously let go of this day, month or year, as the case may be, and you imagine that it is now that day, month or year which you desire to experience. You sense and feel the reality of the desired time by impressing upon yourself the fact that it is now accomplished.

As you sense the naturalness of this time, you begin to feel the thrill of having fully realized that which before you started this psychological journey in time you desired to experience at this time.

With the knowledge of your power to bless, you can open the doors of any prison . . the prison of illness or poverty or of a humdrum existence.

"The Spirit of the Lord God is upon me; because the Lord hath anointed me to preach good tidings unto the meek; he hath sent me to bind up the broken hearted, to proclaim liberty to the captives, and the opening of the prison to them that are bound."

(From Freedom For All)

Neville Goddard - Consciousness: The Giver Of All Gifts

God speaks to man only through the medium of his basic desires. Your desires are determined by your conception of yourself. Of themselves they are neither good or evil.

"I know and am persuaded by the Lord Christ Jesus that there is nothing unclean of itself but to him that seeth anything to be unclean to him it is unclean."

Your desires are the natural and automatic result of your present conception of yourself. God, you unconditioned consciousness, is impersonal and no respecter of persons. Your unconditioned consciousness, God, gives to your conditioned consciousness, man, through the medium of your basic desires that which your conditioned state (your present conception of yourself) believes it needs.

As long as you remain in your present conscious state so long will you continue desiring that which you now desire. Change your conception of yourself and you will automatically change the nature of your desires.

Desires are states of consciousness seeking embodiment. They are formed by man's consciousness and can easily be expressed by the man who has conceived them. Desires are expressed when the man who has conceived them assumes the attitude of mind that would be his if the states desired were already expressed.

Now because desires regardless of their nature can be so easily expressed by fixed attitudes of mind, a word of warning must be given to those who have not yet realized the oneness of life, and who do not know the fundamental truth that consciousness is God, the one and only reality.

This warning was given to man in the famous Golden Rule . . .

"Do unto others that which you would have them do unto you."

You may desire something for yourself or you may desire for another. If your desire concerns another make sure that the thing desired is acceptable to that other. The reason for this warning is that your consciousness is God, the giver of all gifts. Therefore, that which you feel and believe to be true of another is a gift you have given him.

The gift that is not accepted returns to the giver.

Be very sure then that you would love to possess the gift yourself, for if you fix a belief within yourself, as true of another, and he does not accept this state as true of himself, this unaccepted gift will embody itself within your world.

Always hear and accept as true of others that which you would desire for yourself. In so doing you are building heaven on earth.

"Do unto others as you would have them do unto you"

is based upon this law.

Only accept such states as true of others that you would willingly accept as true of yourself that you may constantly create heaven on earth.

Your heaven is defined by the state of consciousness in which you live, which state is made up of all that you accept as true of yourself and true of others. Your immediate environment is defined by your own conception of yourself plus your convictions regarding others which have not been accepted by them.

Your conception of another which is not his conception of himself is a gift returned to you.

Suggestions, like propaganda, are boomerangs unless they are accepted by those to whom they are sent.

So your world is a gift you have given to yourself.

The nature of the gift is determined by your conception of yourself plus the unaccepted gifts you offered others. Make no mistake about this; law is no respecter of persons.

Neville Goddard - Consciousness: The Giver Of All Gifts

Discover the law of self-expression and live by it; then you will be free.

With this understanding of the law, define your desire; know exactly what you want; make certain that it is desirable and acceptable.

The wise and disciplined man sees no barrier to the realization of his desire; he sees nothing to destroy. With a fixed attitude of mind he recognizes that the thing desired is already fully expressed, for he knows that a fixed subjective state, has ways and means of expressing itself, of which no man knows.

> *"Before they ask I have answered."*
>
> *"I have ways ye know not of."*
>
> *"My ways are past finding out."*

The undisciplined man, on the other hand, constantly sees opposition to the fulfillment of his desire, and, because of the frustration, he forms desires of destruction which he firmly believes must be expressed before his basic desire can be realized.

When man discovers this law of one consciousness he will understand the great wisdom of the Golden Rule and so he will live by it and prove to himself that the kingdom of heaven is on earth.

You will realize why you should "do unto others that which you would have them do unto you." You will know why you should live by this Golden Rule because you will discover that it is just good common sense to do so since the rule is based upon life's changeless law and is no respecter of persons.

> Consciousness is the one and only reality.

The world and all within it are states of consciousness objectified. Your world is defined by your conception of yourself, plus your conceptions of others, which are not their conceptions of themselves.

The story of the Passover is to help you turn your back on the limitations of the present and pass over into a better and freer state. The suggestion to

"Follow the man with the pitcher of water"

was given to the disciples to guide them to the last supper or the feast of the Passover. The man with the pitcher of water is the eleventh disciple, Simon of Canaan, the disciplined quality of mind which hears only dignified, noble and kindly states.

The mind that is disciplined to hear only the good, feasts upon good states, and so embodies the good on earth. If you, too, would attend the last supper . . the great feast of the Passover . . then follow this man.

Assume this attitude of mind symbolized as the

"man with the pitcher of water"

and you will live in a world that is really heaven on earth. The feast of the Passover is the secret of changing your consciousness. You turn your attention from your present conception of yourself and assume the consciousness of being that which you want to be, thereby passing from one state to another.

This feat is accomplished with the help of the twelve disciples, which are the twelve disciplined qualities of mind*

*"Your Faith is Your Fortune".

(From Freedom For All)

Neville Goddard - Consciousness: The Giver Of All Gifts

"And Jesus said unto them, Because of your unbelief; for verily I say unto you, if ye have faith as a grain of mustard seed, *ye shall say unto this mountain, remove hence to yonder place; and it shall remove; and nothing shall be impossible unto you."*

This faith of a grain of mustard seed has proved a stumbling block to man. He has been taught to believe that a grain of mustard seed signifies a small degree of faith. So he naturally wonders why he, a mature man, should lack this insignificant measure of faith when so small an amount assures success.

"Faith," he is told, *"is the substance of things hoped for, the evidence of things not seen."*

And again,

"Through faith... the worlds were framed by the word of God, so that things which are seen were not made of things which do appear."

Invisible things were made visible. The grain of mustard seed is not the measure of a small amount of faith. On the contrary, it is the absolute in faith. A mustard seed is conscious of being a mustard seed and a mustard seed alone. It is not aware of any other seed in the world. It is sealed in the conviction that it is a mustard seed in the same manner that the spermatozoa sealed in the womb is conscious of being man and only man.

A grain of mustard seed is truly the measure of faith necessary to accomplish your every objective; but like the mustard seed you too must lose yourself in the consciousness of being only the thing desired.

You abide within this sealed state until it bursts itself and reveals your conscious claim.

Faith is feeling or living in the consciousness of being the thing desired; faith is the secret of creation, the VAU in the divine name JOD HE VAU HE; faith is the Ham in the family of Noah; faith is the sense of feeling by which Isaac blessed and made real his son Jacob.

By faith, God (your consciousness), calleth things that are not seen as though they were and makes them seen.

It is faith which enables you to become conscious of being the thing desired; again, it is faith which seals you in this conscious state until your invisible claim ripens to maturity and expresses itself, is made visible. Faith or feeling is the secret of this appropriation. Through feeling, the consciousness desiring is joined to the thing desired.

How would you feel if you were that which you desire to be?

Wear the mood, this feeling that would be yours if you were already that which you desire to be; and in a little while you will be sealed in the belief that you are. Then without effort this invisible state will objectify itself; the invisible will be made visible.

If you had the faith of a grain of mustard seed, you would this day, through the magical substance of feeling, seal yourself in the consciousness of being that which you desire to be. In this mental stillness or tomblike state you would remain, confident that you need no one to roll away the stone, for all the mountains, stones and inhabitants of earth are nothing in your sight.

That which you now recognize to be true of yourself (this present conscious state) will do according to its nature among all the inhabitants of earth, and none can stay its hand or say unto it,

"What doest Thou?"

None can stop this conscious state in which you are sealed, from embodying itself, nor question its right to be.

This conscious state when properly sealed by faith is a Word of God, I AM, for the man so seated is saying, "I AM so and so," and the Word of God (my fixed conscious state) is spirit and cannot return unto me void but must accomplish whereunto it is sent. God's word (your conscious state) must embody itself that you may know:

> *"I AM the Lord... there is no God beside Me;"*
> *"The Word was made flesh and dwelt among us;"*

> and

> *"He sent His word and healed him."*

You too can send your word, God's Word, and heal a friend. Is there something that you would like to hear of a friend? Define this something that you know he would love to be or to possess. Now with your desire properly defined you have a Word of God.

To send this Word on its way, to speak this Word into being, you simply do this.

Sit quietly where you are and assume the mental attitude of listening; recall your friend's voice; with this familiar voice established in your consciousness, imagine that you are actually hearing his voice and that he is telling you that he is or has that which you wanted him to be or to have.

Impress upon your consciousness the fact that you actually heard him and that he told you what you wanted to hear; feel the thrill of having heard. Then drop it completely.

This is the mystic's secret of sending words into expression, of making the word flesh.

You form within yourself the word, the thing you want to hear; then you listen, and tell it to yourself.

> *"Speak, Lord, for thy servant heareth."*

Your consciousness is the Lord speaking through the familiar voice of a friend and impressing on yourself that which you desire to hear. This self-impregnation, the state impressed upon yourself, the Word, has ways and means of expressing itself of which no man knows.

As you succeed in making the impression you will be unmoved by appearances for this self-impression is sealed as a grain of mustard seed and will in due season mature to its full expression.

(From Freedom For All)

Neville Goddard - Consciousness: The Giver Of All Gifts

DUAL NATURE OF CONSCIOUSNESS

A clear concept of the dual nature of man's consciousness must be the basis of all true prayer.

Consciousness includes a subconscious as well as a conscious part. The infinitely greater part of consciousness lies below the sphere of objective consciousness. The subconscious is the most important part of consciousness. It is the cause of voluntary action. The subconscious is what a man is. The conscious is what a man knows.

"I and my Father are one but my Father is greater than I."

The conscious and subconscious are one, but the subconscious is greater than the conscious.

*"I of myself can do nothing, the Father within
me He doeth the work."*

I, objective consciousness, of myself can do nothing; the Father, the subconscious, He doeth the work. The subconscious is that in which everything is known, in which everything is possible, to which everything goes, from which everything comes, which belongs to all, to which all have access.

What we are conscious of is constructed out of what we are not conscious of. Not only do our subconscious assumptions influence our behavior but they also fashion the pattern of our objective existence. They alone have the power to say,

*"Let us make man . . objective manifestations . . in
our image, after our likeness."*

The whole of creation is asleep within the deep of man and is awakened to objective existence by his subconscious assumptions.

Within that blankness we call sleep there is a consciousness in unsleeping vigilance, and while the body sleeps this unsleeping being releases from the treasure house of eternity the subconscious assumptions of man.

Prayer is the key which unlocks the infinite storehouse.

"Prove me now herewith, saith the Lord of hosts, if I will not open you the windows of heaven, and pour you out a blessing, that there shall not be room enough to receive it."

Prayer modifies or completely changes our subconscious assumptions, and a change of assumption is a change of expression.

The conscious mind reasons inductively from observation, experience and education. It therefore finds it difficult to believe what the five senses and inductive reason deny.

The subconscious reasons deductively and is never concerned with the truth or falsity of the premise, but proceeds on the assumption of the correctness of the premise and objectifies results which are consistent with the premise.

This distinction must be clearly seen by all who would master the art of praying.

No true grasp of the science of prayer can be really obtained until the laws governing the dual nature of consciousness are understood and the importance of the subconscious realized.

Prayer .. the art of believing what is denied by the senses .. deals almost entirely with the subconscious. Through prayer, the subconscious is suggested, into acceptance of the wish fulfilled, and, reasoning deductively, logically unfolds it to its legitimate end.

"Far greater is He that is in you than he that is in the world."

The subjective mind is the diffused consciousness that animates the world; it is the spirit that giveth life. In all substance, is a single soul .. subjective mind. Through all creation runs this one unbroken subjective mind.

Neville Goddard - Consciousness: The Giver Of All Gifts

Thought and feeling fused into beliefs impress modifications upon it, charge it with a mission, which mission it faithfully executes. The conscious mind originates premises. The subjective mind unfolds them to their logical ends.

Were the subjective mind not so limited in its initiative power of reasoning, objective man could not be held responsible for his actions in the world. Man transmits ideas to the subconscious through his feelings. The subconscious transmits ideas from mind to mind through telepathy.

Your unexpressed convictions of others are transmitted to them without their conscious knowledge or consent, and if subconsciously accepted by them will influence their behavior.

The only ideas they subconsciously reject are your ideas of them which they could not wish to be true of anyone. Whatever they could wish for others can be believed of them, and by the law of belief which governs subjective reasoning they are compelled to subjectively accept, and therefore objectively express, accordingly.

The subjective mind is completely controlled by suggestion.

Ideas are best suggested when the objective mind is partly subjective, that is, when the objective senses are diminished or held in abeyance. This partly subjective state can best be described as controlled reverie, wherein the mind is passive but capable of functioning with absorption. It is a concentration of attention.

There must be no conflict in your mind when you are praying. Turn from what is to what ought to be. Assume the mood of fulfilled desire, and by the universal law of reversibility you will realize your desire.

(From Prayer, The Art Of Believing)

IMAGINATION AND FAITH

Prayers are not successfully made unless there is a rapport between the conscious and subconscious mind of the operator. This is done through imagination and faith.

By the power of imagination all men, certainly imaginative men, are forever casting forth enchantments, and all men, especially unimaginative men, are continually passing under their power.

Can we ever be certain that it was not our mother while darning our socks who began that subtle change in our minds? If I can unintentionally cast an enchantment over persons, there is no reason to doubt that I am able to cast intentionally a far stronger enchantment.

Everything, that can be seen, touched, explained, argued over, is to the imaginative man nothing more than a means, for he functions, by reason of his controlled imagination, in the deep of himself where every idea exists in itself and not in relation to something else. In him there is no need for the restraints of reason. For the only restraint he can obey is the mysterious instinct that teaches him to eliminate all moods other than the mood of the fulfilled desire.

Imagination and faith are the only faculties of the mind needed to create objective conditions.

The faith required for the successful operation of the law of consciousness is a purely subjective faith and is attainable upon the cessation of active opposition on the part of the objective mind of the operator.

It depends on your ability to feel and accept as true what your objective senses deny.

Neither the passivity of the subject nor his conscious agreement with your suggestion is necessary, for without his consent or knowledge he can be given a subjective order which he must objectively express. It is a fundamental law of consciousness that by telepathy we can have immediate communion with another.

To establish rapport you call the subject mentally. Focus your attention on him and mentally shout his name just as you would to attract the attention of anyone. Imagine that he answered, and mentally hear his voice. Represent him to yourself inwardly in the state you want him to obtain. Then imagine that he is telling you in the tones of ordinary conversation what you want to hear. Mentally answer him. Tell him of your joy in witnessing his good fortune.

Having mentally heard with all the distinctness of reality that which you wanted to hear and having thrilled to the news heard, return to objective consciousness. Your subjective conversation must awaken what it affirmed.

> *"Thou shalt decree a thing and it shall be established unto thee."*

It is not a strong will that sends the subjective word on its mission, so much as it is clear thinking and feeling, the truth of the state affirmed. When belief and will are in conflict, belief invariably wins.

> *"Not by might, nor by power, but by my spirit, saith the Lord of hosts."*

It is not what you want that you attract; you attract what you believe to be true.

Therefore, get into the spirit of these mental conversations and give them the same degree of reality that you would a telephone conversation.

> *"If thou canst believe, all things are possible to him that believeth. Therefore, I say unto you, what things soever you desire, when you pray, believe that ye received them, and ye shall have them."*

The acceptance of the end wills the means. And the wisest reflection could not devise more effective means than those which are willed by the acceptance of the end. Mentally talk to your friends as though your desires for them were already realized.

Imagination is the beginning of the growth of all forms, and faith is the substance out of which they are formed.

By imagination, that which exists in latency or is asleep within the deep of consciousness is awakened and is given form.

The cures attributed to the influence of certain medicines, relics and places are the effects of imagination and faith. The curative power is not in the spirit that is in them, it is in the spirit in which they are accepted.

> *"The letter killeth, but the spirit giveth life."*

The subjective mind is completely controlled by suggestion, so, whether the object of your faith be true or false, you will get the same results.

There is nothing unsound in the theory of medicine or in the claims of priesthood for their relics and holy places. The subjective mind of the patient accepts the suggestion of health conditioned on such states, and as soon as these conditions are met proceeds to realize health.

> *"According to your faith be it done unto you for all things are possible to him that believeth."*

Confident expectation of a state is the most potent means of bringing it about. The confident expectation of a cure does that which no medical treatment can accomplish.

Failure is always due to an antagonistic auto-suggestion by the patient, arising from objective doubt of the power of medicine or relic, or from doubt of the truth of the theory. Many of us, either from too little emotion or too much intellect, both of which are stumbling blocks in the way or prayer, cannot believe that which our sense deny.

To force ourselves to believe, will end in greater doubt. To avoid such counter-suggestions the patient should be unaware, objectively, of the suggestions which are made to him.

The most effective method of healing or influencing the behavior of others consists in what is known as "the silent or absent treatment." When the subject is unaware, objectively, of the suggestion given him there is no possibility of him setting up an antagonistic belief. It is not necessary that the patient know, objectively, that anything is being done for him.

From what is known of the subjective and objective processes of reasoning, it is better that he should not know objectively of that which is being done for him. The more completely the objective mind is kept in ignorance of the suggestion, the better will the subjective mind perform its functions.

The subject subconsciously accepts the suggestion and thinks he originates it, proving the truth of Spinoza's dictum, that we know not the causes that determine our actions.

The subconscious mind is the universal conductor which the operator modifies with his thoughts and feelings. Visible states are either the vibratory effects of subconscious vibrations within you or they are vibratory causes of the corresponding vibrations within you. A disciplined man never permits them to be causes unless they awaken in him the desirable states of consciousness.

(From Prayer, The Art Of Believing)

LAW OF THOUGHT TRANSMISSION
(Entire Chapter From Prayer, The Art Of Believing)

"He sent his word and healed them, and delivered them from their destructions."

He transmitted the consciousness of health and awoke its vibratory correlate in the one toward whom it was directed. He mentally represented the subject to himself in a state of health and imagined he heard the subject confirm it.

"For no word of God shall be void of power; therefore hold fast the pattern of healthful words which thou has heard."

To pray successfully you must have clearly defined objectives. You must know what you want before you can ask for it. You must know what you want before you can feel that you have it, and prayer is the feeling of the fulfilled desire.

It does not matter what it is you seek in prayer, or where it is, or whom it concerns.

You have nothing to do but convince yourself of the truth of that which you desire to see manifested.

When you emerge from prayer, you no longer seek, for you have, if you have prayed correctly, subconsciously assumed the reality of the state sought, and by the law of reversibility your subconscious must objectify that which it affirms.

You must have a conductor to transmit a force. You may employ a wire, a jet of water, a current of air, a ray of light or any intermediary whatsoever.

The principle of the photophone or the transmission of the voice by light will help you to understand thought transmission, or the sending of a word to heal another.
There is a strong analogy between a spoken voice and a mental voice. To think is to speak low, to speak is to think aloud.

Neville Goddard - Consciousness: The Giver Of All Gifts

The principle of the photophone is this:

A ray of light is reflected by a mirror and projected to a receiver at a distant point. Back of the mirror is a mouthpiece. By speaking into the mouthpiece you cause the mirror to vibrate. A vibrating mirror modifies the light reflected on it. The modified light has your speech to carry, not as speech, but as represented in its mechanical correlate. It reaches the distant station and impinges on a disc within the receiver; it causes the disc to vibrate according to the modification it undergoes . . and it reproduces your voice.

"I AM the light of the world."

I AM, the knowledge that I exist, is a light by means of which what passes in my mind is rendered visible.

Memory, or my ability to mentally see what is objectively present, proves that my mind is a mirror, so sensitive a mirror that it can reflect a thought. The perception of an image in memory in no way differs as a visual act from the perception of my image in a mirror.

The same principle of seeing is involved in both.

Your consciousness is the light reflected on the mirror of your mind and projected in space to the one of whom you think. By mentally speaking to the subjective image in your mind you cause the mirror of your mind to vibrate.

Your vibrating mind modifies the light of consciousness reflected on it. The modified light of consciousness reaches the one toward whom it is directed and impinges on the mirror of his mind; it causes his mind to vibrate according to the modification it undergoes. Thus, it reproduces in him what was mentally affirmed by you.

Your beliefs, your fixed attitudes of mind, constantly modify your consciousness, as it is reflected on the mirror of your mind.

Neville Goddard - Consciousness: The Giver Of All Gifts

Your consciousness, modified by your beliefs, objectifies itself in the conditions of your world.

To change your world, you must first change your conception of it.

To change a man, you must change your conception of him. You must first believe him to be the man you want him to be and mentally talk to him as though he were.

All men are sufficiently sensitive to reproduce your beliefs of them.

Therefore, if your word is not reproduced visibly in him toward whom it is sent, the cause is to be found in you, not in the subject.

As soon as you believe in the truth of the state affirmed, results follow. Everyone can be transformed; every thought can be transmitted; every thought can be visibly embodied.

Subjective words . . subconscious assumptions . . awaken what they affirm.

> They are living and active and
>
> *"shall not return unto me void,*
> *but shall accomplish that which I please,*
> *and shall prosper in the thing whereto I sent them."*

They are endowed with the intelligence pertaining to their mission and will persist until the object of their existence is realized; they persist until they awaken the vibratory correlates of themselves, within the one toward whom they are directed, but the moment the object of their creation is accomplished they cease to be.

The word spoken subjectively in quiet confidence will always awaken a corresponding state in the one in whom it was spoken; but the moment its task is accomplished it ceases to be, permitting the one in whom the state is realized to remain in the consciousness of the state affirmed or to return to his former state.

Whatever state has your attention holds your life. Therefore, to become attentive to a former state is to return to that condition.

> *"Remember not the former things, neither consider things of old."*

Nothing can be added to man, for the whole of creation is already perfected in him.

> *"The kingdom of heaven is within you."*

"Man can receive nothing, except it be given him from heaven."

> Heaven is your subconsciousness.

Not even a sunburn is given from without. The rays without only awaken corresponding rays within. Were the burning rays not contained within man, all the concentrated rays in the universe could not burn him.

Were the tones of health not contained within the consciousness of the one whom they are affirmed, they could not be vibrated by the word which is sent. You do not really give to another, you resurrect that which is asleep within him.

> *"The damsel is not dead, but sleepeth."*

Death is merely a sleeping and forgetting. Age and decay are the sleep, not death, of youth and health.

> Recognition of a state vibrates or awakens it.

Distance, as it is cognized by your objective senses, does not exist for the subjective mind.

> *"If I take the wings of the morning, and*
> *dwell in the uttermost parts of the sea;*

even there shall thy hand lead me."

Time and space are conditions of thought; the imagination can transcend them and move in a psychological time and space. Although physically separated from a place by thousands of miles, you can mentally live in the distant place as though it were here.

Your imagination can easily transform winter into summer, New York into Florida, and so on.

Whether the object of your desire be near or far, results will be the same. Subjectively, the object of your desire is never far off; its intense nearness makes it remote from observation of the senses. It dwells in consciousness, and consciousness is closer than breathing and nearer than hands and feet.

Consciousness is the one and only reality. All phenomena are formed of the same substance vibrating at different rates. Out of consciousness, I as man came, and to consciousness, I as man return.

In consciousness all states exist subjectively, and are awakened to their objective existence by belief. The only thing that prevents us from making a successful subjective impression on one at a great distance, or transforming there into here, is our habit of regarding space as an obstacle.

A friend a thousand miles away is rooted in your consciousness through your fixed ideas of him. To think of him and represent him to yourself inwardly in the state you desire him to be, confident that this subjective image is as true as it were already objectified, awakens in him a corresponding state which he must objectify.
The results will be as obvious as the cause was hidden. The subject will express the awakened state within him and remain unaware of the true cause of his action.

Your illusion of free will is but ignorance of the causes which make you act. Prayers depend upon your attitude of mind for their success and not upon the attitude of the subject.

Neville Goddard - Consciousness: The Giver Of All Gifts

The subject has no power to resist your controlled subjective ideas of him unless the state affirmed by you, to be true of him, is a state he is incapable of wishing as true of another. In that case it returns to you, the sender, and will realize itself in you.

Provided the idea is acceptable, success depends entirely on the operator not upon the subject who, like compass needles on their pivots, are quite indifferent as to what direction you choose to give them. If your fixed idea is not subjectively accepted by the one toward whom it is directed, it rebounds to you from whom it came.

> *"Who is he that will harm you, if ye be followers of that which is good? I have been young, and now am old; yet have I not seen the righteous forsaken, nor his seed begging bread."*

> *"There shall no evil happen to the just."*

Nothing befalls us that is not of the nature of ourselves.

A person who directs a malicious thought to another will be injured by its rebound if he fails to get subconscious acceptance of the other.

> *"As ye sow, so shall ye reap."*

Furthermore, what you can wish and believe of another can be wished and believed of you, and you have no power to reject it if the one who desires it for you accepts it as true of you.

The only power to reject a subjective word is to be incapable of wishing a similar state of another . . to give, presupposes the ability to receive.

The possibility to impress an idea upon another mind presupposes the ability of that mind to receive that impression. Fools exploit the world; the wise transfigure it.

Neville Goddard - Consciousness: The Giver Of All Gifts

It is the highest wisdom to know that in the living universe there is no destiny other than that created out of imagination of man.

There is no influence outside of the mind of man.

"Whatsoever things are lovely, whatsoever are of good report; if there be any virtue and if there be any praise, think on these things."

Never accept as true of others what you would not want to be true of you. To awaken a state within another it must first be awake within you. The state you would transmit to another can only be transmitted, if it is believed by you.

Therefore to give is to receive.

You cannot give what you do not have and you have only what you believe.

So to believe a state as true of another not only awakens that state within the other but it makes it alive within you.

You are what you believe.

"Give and ye shall receive, full measure, pressed down and running over."

Giving is simply believing, for what you truly believe of others you will awaken within them.

The vibratory state transmitted by your belief persists until it awakens its corresponding vibration in him of whom it is believed.

But before it can be transmitted it must first be awake within the transmitter.

Whatever is awake within your consciousness, you are. Whether the belief pertains to self or another does not matter, for the believer is defined by the sum total of his beliefs or subconscious assumptions.

Neville Goddard - Consciousness: The Giver Of All Gifts

"As a man thinketh in his heart"

in the deep subconscious of himself

"so is he."

Disregard appearances and subjectively affirm as true that which you wish to be true.

This awakens in you the tone of the state affirmed which in turn realizes itself in you and in the one of whom it is affirmed.

"Give and ye shall receive."

Beliefs invariably awaken what they affirm.

(From Prayer, The Art Of Believing)

Metaphysical / Law of Attraction Books

David Allen - The Power of I AM (2014), The Power of I AM - Volume 2 (2015) , The Power of I AM - Volume 3 (2017)

David Allen - The Creative Power of Thought, Man's Greatest Discovery (2017)

David Allen - The Secrets, Mysteries & Powers of The Subconscious Mind (2017)

David Allen - The Money Bible - The Secrets of Attracting Prosperity (2017)

David Allen - Your Faith Is Your Fortune, Your Unlimited Power (2018)

David Allen - ASKffirmations: Questions That Create Reality

The Neville Goddard Collection (All 10 of his books plus 2 Lecture series) (2016)

Neville Goddard - Assumptions Harden Into Facts: The Book (2016)

Neville Goddard - Imagination: The Redemptive Power in Man (2016)

Neville Goddard - The World is At Your Command - The Very Best of Neville Goddard (2017)

Neville Goddard - Imagining Creates Reality - 365 Mystical Daily Quotes (2017)

Neville Goddard's Interpretation of Scripture (2018)

The Definitive Christian D. Larson Collection (6 Volumes, 30 books) (2014)

David Allen - The Within Creates The Without: Creating Our Lives By Design: Daily Meditations

David Allen - The Creative Power Of Mind: Daily Meditations For A Better Life

Be sure to check out NevilleGoddardBooks.com for thousands of free eBooks on metaphysics.

www.ingramcontent.com/pod-product-compliance
Lightning Source LLC
Chambersburg PA
CBHW020424010526
44118CB00010B/414